Authors! The Quick Book to Business Method™

Ellen Finkelstein and Connie Ragen Green

Hunter's Moon Publishing
http://HuntersMoonPublishing.com

Hunter's Moon Publishing - Connie Ragen Green
P.O. Box 3295
Santa Barbara, CA 93180-3295

Ellen Finkelstein - ChangetheWorldMarketing.com
Connie Ragen Green - ConnieRagenGreen.com

As the purchaser of this book we (Connie Ragen Green and Ellen Finkelstein) wish to gift you one of the Modules from our ongoing training course. Authors! The Quick Book to Business Method™ at:
https://OnlineWritingProfits.com/sample

What People Are Saying

"Connie Ragen Green is a force to be reckoned with. She teaches from her heart and encourages her students to take action quickly. I now have the confidence to move forward with my business that is based on my new book."

~ Douglas Glatthorn

"Every now and then you find someone with the perfect balance of skill, knowledge and passion for what they do. You find those qualities in Ellen Finkelstein. Her expertise in book writing has made a huge difference in my life. I have no qualms in recommending Ellen to any who want to grow their business."

~ Ron Price

Download a full Module from our popular course at:
https://OnlineWritingProfits.com/sample

This is our Module on Creating an Online Course based on your book.

Table of Contents

Dedication

This book is dedicated to the authors and entrepreneurs we have individually and together worked with over the years. You are dedicated to sharing your message with the world and have decided to use your book as a way to reach the people who will most benefit from what you have to share.

Authors! The Quick Book to Business Method™

Turning Your Book into an Ongoing Revenue Stream

Ellen Finkelstein & Connie Ragen Green

Preface

From Connie Ragen Green:

When Ellen Finkelstein first approached me about writing a book on our topic of teaching authors how to turn their book into a business, I was both surprised and honored. Ellen is one of the smartest and most business savvy entrepreneurs and authors working online today.

We've been co-teaching a course on this topic for more than a year now, but the idea of co-authoring with someone of her caliber was daunting. I spent a week thinking this through, addressing personal fears and trepidations, and finally was able to shift my mindset to a place where writing a book with Ellen made perfect sense to me.

From Ellen Finkelstein:

When Connie Ragen Green first approached me to talk about working together on our Authors course, I was also surprised and honored. Connie is one of the most successful online entrepreneurs I know. And more than that, her success comes from determination, smarts, and expertise, but mostly a sincere desire to help people earn a good living online. I so admire her!

I was worried that she wouldn't consider me worthwhile to partner with, but she has been generous and easy to work with. I feel so lucky!

From both of us:

The concept of taking your book and turning it into a business is one that can change everything you are working towards in your life and business. Imagine being able to write a book on your topic and in the area of your expertise and then use that single document as the basis for additional trainings and programs and courses and more.

The goal and intention of this work is to share and inform you of what is possible when you write your book and turn it into an income stream. There are so many possibilities and this model can take you places you did not previously know even existed.

Perhaps you already teach a live or virtual course on your topic and you are now writing a book to go along with it. This is perfectly acceptable and will bring you excellent results because there is no right or wrong way to go about this.

Maybe you are a public speaker and wrote your book years ago. Your business model may include coaching in person to one or many. This book could help you to create your online course and begin conducting much of your coaching virtually, freeing up more time to do other things in your life.

Wherever you are at the present time and whatever you have done in years past will all be valuable experience as you move into the future, implementing and applying the principles, concepts, and strategies in the "Authors! The Quick Book to Business Method™" you will learn from Ellen and me within these pages.

Introduction

"Without continual growth and progress, such words as improvement, achievement, and success have no meaning."

~ Benjamin Franklin

We have laid out this book in the most direct way possible for you to be able to learn, implement, and achieve your goals by turning your book into a business.

In Part I, Connie begins by discussing authorship as a business model, which is the focus of this book. Then she moves on to other authors who have successfully used this model to grow their own businesses.

In Part II, Ellen explains how to use a book as part of a "funnel" that includes other products and courses and how to connect all of the pieces.

In Part III, Connie covers how to turn your book into a course that can bring in more income than a book alone.

In Part IV, Ellen talks about how to use storytelling to engage your readers, customers, and clients.

———————————————————————————

We also have a gift for you from the course we teach together—one of the Modules from our ongoing training course. Authors! The Quick Book to Business Method™ at:
www.OnlineWritingProfits.com/sample

———————————————————————————

Part I

Authorship as a Business Model

"If you are patient...and wait long enough...
Nothing will happen."
~ Jim Davis, creator of the Garfield comic strip series

The concept and idea of turning your book into a business is a relatively new one. I first became aware of this as a business model in the early 1990s. In this section we will take a closer look at some authors who have done this successfully. You may recognize at least some of the names, as these people have become household names over time.

Later on we'll share exactly how you can get started with this model for your own book, but for now simply hold the vision of what your life and business would look like if you follow our "Authors! Quick Book to Business Method™" as your own system for success.

Imagine if you will that you have written the book based on an idea that may have been inside of you for years. This book shares the message of what you wish to share with others all around the world. You know down deep there are many people, too numerous to count who will benefit from your stories, experiences, and ideas if only they could hear them from you.

Your book will open the door to reaching the exact people you believe want and need your message in order to change their lives and live up to their God given potential.

Now imagine your book not only reaching the right people all over the world, but also becoming a source of income for you so that you can devote more time to spreading your message and changing people's lives.

This is the precept upon which this book is based; as an author you will be able to quickly use your book as the foundation of a business where you decide how best to get your thoughts, ideas, and message into the hands, both virtually and literally of the people who can only hear it from you.

In the first chapter I (Connie) discuss the history of this "book to business" model. Knowing how something began and then evolved is crucial to a full understanding of what you will be working towards, I believe.

In Chapter 2 I share the stories of other authors who have used this model successfully. This information will be helpful in that the idea for what Ellen and I are sharing with you here is a viable one for any topic, niche, and area of expertise.

Then in Chapter 3 I explain why and how to use an outline. When you start with an outline, you'll be able to write your book most quickly and effortlessly.

CHAPTER 1

The History of the Book to Business Model

I can remember when I first thought of authorship as a business model. The author was John Gray, and he had just published his now famous book, *Men Are From Mars, Women Are From Venus: A Practical Guide for Improving Communication and Getting What You Want in Your Relationship*. The year was 1992 and the title took the world by storm.

Dr. Gray had worked as a psychologist for a number of years before penning this first book. Once it took off in the bookstores he began appearing on television and was interviewed on radio shows across the land, leaving his therapy practice behind.

If you were alive during this period there was not much chance you were not aware of the name John Gray and the topic of men and women being even more different than we had previously believed them to be. And you absolutely had to have your own copy of his book.

Remember this was long before the internet or even the World Wide Web was a part of our daily lives, so in retrospect this was all in slow motion compared to what would happen today.

Almost immediately upon becoming a household name, at least in North America Dr. Gray began hosting live events and workshops where he would further explain his book. The key phrase here is "further explain" his book because he had already shared every detail of his precept, based on decades of study and work with his patients, within its pages. Later I would understand this concept of authors being able to earn much more income from explaining their books than from simply selling them.

Now these were the days when you had to have an agent and a traditional publishing company to get your book into bookstores and in the news. This book was published by Harper Collins and they did an excellent job of coordinating their public relations team. They did this in a way that could maximize sales by putting Dr. Gray in front of as many people as possible during that important ninety day window of opportunity after a book is first released and available in bookstores. He appeared on television and radio, as well as being interviewed in newspapers and magazine.

Over the next year he created courses and programs and outlined his next book, making Dr. John Gray PhD a valuable commodity. Everyone was interested at some level and the idea that we could experience a professional tour through the hearts and minds of people of the opposite sex was too tempting to pass up.

Publishing a book each year for the following nine years added to his credibility. If you had any interest in relationships on any level this author was top of mind and a conversational topic between friends of the same sex and acquaintances of the opposite sex. Overnight millions of people around the world became voyeurs in this arena.

All of a sudden we were thrust into a new world where books from this author were reference guides to the masses. Dr. Gray's radio and television appearances, along with his in person events were similar to getting your own PhD in this area and educating yourself in a way that had never been done up until this time.

Over these past twenty-five years or so this has led to infomercials, audiotapes and videotapes, a CD-ROM, weekend seminars and retreats, theme vacations, a one-man Broadway show, a TV sitcom, a movie contract with 20th Century Fox, protein powder, and hundreds of vitamins and supplements. This is an extreme example of how you, using the book to business model we are sharing with you in this book, could potentially become a cottage industry of your own.

John Gray is someone I had the pleasure of sharing the stage with in London in 2012. He spoke openly about his education and how everyone assumes he is a Harvard or other Ivy League graduate who went into private practice before becoming an author, speaker, and businessman.

The truth is that he received both his bachelor's and master's degrees in the Science of Creative Intelligence, though the Maharishi International University in Fairfield, Iowa. He received an unaccredited PhD degree by correspondence in 1982 from the now defunct Columbia Pacific University (CPU) in northern California, upon completion of a correspondence course. Even a family therapist with less than stellar credentials can turn a book into a lucrative business.

Let's move forward to see how others have replicated this proven strategy in a similar way in the years since then.

CHAPTER 2

Other Authors Who Have Used This Method

There are also many other authors who have done the same thing, or something similar to what I described in the previous chapter in terms of allowing their writing to carry them to new heights and build their empire. Let's take a closer look at a few of these people to better understand this concept of turning your book into a business with a viable income stream.

J.K. Rowling

"It's impossible to live without failing at something, unless you live so cautiously that you might as well have not lived at all."

~ J.K. Rowling

Joanne Kathleen Rowling, is a British novelist, screenwriter, philanthropist, and film producer. Under the pen names J.K. Rowling and Robert Galbraith she is best known for creating the *Harry Potter* series of books and a series of crime fiction novels, respectively.

She lived a rags-to-riches story of being on welfare during the entire seven year period during which she was writing the first book in the *Harry Potter* series, and then going on to become the first billionaire author in the world.

Her rise to fame and fortune was fraught with twists and turns that could not have been predicted. She credits these life experiences as being the ones that kept her focused on her writing and her goals for after the first book was finally written and accepted by a publisher.

Her first novel in the series, *Harry Potter and the Philosopher's Stone*, was published in 1997. Six sequels followed, with the last in the series being published in 2007. During this time and going forward Rowling has lived an extraordinary life.

Rowling had gained some creative control on the Harry Potter films, reviewing all the scripts as well as acting as a producer on the final two-part installment, *Harry Potter and the Deathly Hallows*. This in and of itself is a unique position to be in as an author.

Warner Bros. studios followed Rowling's requests in regards to the shooting of the Harry Potter films. One of her principal stipulations that was not negotiable was the films be shot in Britain with an all-British cast, which was generally adhered to and accepted by her agent. Rowling also demanded that Coca-Cola, the victor in the race to tie in their products to the film series, donate $18 million to the American charity "Reading is Fundamental," as well as several community charity programs.

Her philanthropy is aimed at helping a number of causes, including anti-poverty and children's welfare. Rowling has also contributed a significant amount of money and support for research and treatment of multiple sclerosis, from which her mother suffered before her death in 1990.

Tim Ferriss

"A person's success in life can usually
be measured by the number of uncomfortable
conversations he or she is willing to have."
~ Tim Ferriss

Tim Ferriss is an author, entrepreneur and startup investor for early-stage tech companies. In 2001, he founded BrainQUICKEN and sold the company to a London-based private equity firm a decade later. His now legendary first book, *The 4-Hour Workweek* was mostly based on this experience. In it he chronicles the journey of entrepreneurs who are able to create the life they are dreaming of using something he popularized called "lifestyle design."

This was followed up by four additional books, including *The 4-Hour Body: An Uncommon Guide to Rapid Fat-Loss, Incredible Sex, and Becoming Superhuman, The 4-Hour Chef: The Simple Path to Cooking Like a Pro, Learning Anything, and Living the Good Life, Tools of Titans: The Tactics, Routines, and Habits of Billionaires, Icons, and World-Class Performers*, and *Tribe of Mentors: Short Life Advice from the Best in the World*. There are other books as well, and they have been translated into more than thirty languages.

Even though Ferriss experienced great success in working with startups and angel investing, he walked away from that world in 2015 and prefers to be known as an author, podcaster, and television show host because this is where he can have the greatest impact.

His podcast is titled "The Tim Ferriss Show" and had been downloaded more than three hundred million times as of this writing.

In 2008 he made the foray into television with a pilot on the History Channel called Trial by Fire. The goal was for him to learn something in one week that would typically take years to learn. There was another television show he created and produced on CNN's Headline News in 2013 but it was not shown in its entirety to the public viewing audience. He is working on making these episodes available on some platform in the near future.

It's important to point out that Ferriss, like all of the authors I am sharing with you who have turned their books into a business did so by focusing on what they loved, excelled at on many levels, and wanted to be known as in the public arena. In this case Tim Ferriss is known as someone who is physically and mentally strong and who is willing to be a human guinea pig for the purpose of uncovering new methods for improving the human condition.

Suze Orman

> *"A big part of financial freedom is having your heart and mind free from worry about the what-ifs of life."*
>
> *~ Suze Orman*

Financial advisor Suze Orman was born into humble beginnings and worked full time as a waitress until she was almost thirty years old. She then decided she wanted to open up her own restaurant. After losing over fifty thousand dollars (borrowed from close friend) in an unwise options trading investment, she decided to devote her time and energy to a career this field to learn more about money and investing for herself.

In 1987 she published a booklet, "The Facts on Single Premium Whole Life," which compared single-premium whole life, universal life, and single-premium deferred annuities; she distributed copies of the booklet for free to anyone who requested one. This was when she realized that writing about her business was very good for business growth.

Between 1995 and 2001 Suze published four books based on what she had learned at the brokerage firms. These included *You've Earned It Don't Lose It* in 1995, *The 9 Steps to Financial Freedom* in 1997, *The Courage to be Rich* in 1999), and *The Road to Wealth* in 2001.

These books were so well received in the United States they led to *The Suze Orman Show* on network television in 2002. When she was a guest on *The Oprah Winfrey Show* she gave away a digital copy of *Women and Money* which resulted in more than two million downloads during the next seven days.

Over the years she has created a library of products aimed at helping the everyday person learn more about handling and managing their money. In 2012 she introduced a prepaid debit card, backed by Bancorp Bank, aimed at budget-challenged consumers. This program was intended to help the "unbanked" in America to build their credit rating but did not succeed for a variety of reasons and was shut down in 2014. Her website lists dozens of books, CDs, DVDs, online courses, and financial kits for almost every area of personal finance.

Suze Orman is the perfect example of someone with a powerful message who is devoting her life to getting that message out to the tens of millions of people who need to hear it most, and would benefit from receiving it directly from her.

Bill Phillips

"The difference between who you are and who you want to be, is what you do."

~ Bill Phillips

Bill Phillips started out as a bodybuilder while still in his teens, and as a result was encouraged to study exercise physiology, sports nutrition, and steroid chemistry while in college at the University of Colorado at Denver.

He then moved back home to launch Mile High Publishing and created a short newsletter that he printed in his mother's garage. Funded with $180 he had made from mowing lawns, its original name was The Anabolic Reference Update. Within five years Bill began working with doctors and research scientists in Colorado to develop performance nutrition products that could help athletes get better muscle-building and fat-burning effects from their workouts without the use of steroids and other harmful drugs.

His first book, *Body for Life* was published in 1999 and within a year more than three million copies had been sold. It has now been translated into twenty-four languages. He followed this up with *Eating for Life* in 2003.

Bill's business includes health and fitness camps and retreats as well as protein powder he sources from New Zealand and nutritional supplements.

I have been to Bill's Transformation Camp at his training center in Golden, Colorado twice, and worked out side by side with him and a dozen others who are interested in learning more about what he has discovered about nutrition and exercise physiology over the past thirty years.

Keep in mind that I have just shared a snippet about the people chosen to be included here. To learn more about them and how they used a book to help catapult them to massive success please take a look at their books and websites.

CHAPTER 3

Outlining Your Non-Fiction Book

Writing a book is somewhat like putting the pieces of a 5000-piece jigsaw puzzle together. I was gifted one of the Sistine Chapel several years ago and encountered difficulty getting started because there were so many options as to where to begin. A puzzle or a book can be completed more easily and with greater impact to those who come upon the final product depending upon how you begin and the path you follow through to the last piece or the final word.

Sort through the five thousand pieces you have in front of you, use two fingers to slide the edge pieces out of the pile and over to the side and you are left with a kaleidoscope of colors in all shapes and sizes that have little rhyme or reason.

Take the alternate tack of searching through the full pile of pieces for those belonging to one image or section of the puzzle and you are left with everything else in disarray.

In either case you still have the front of the box to refer to as you make your way along the road from connecting two puzzle pieces at the beginning all the way to inserting the final piece at the end. With your book you have no image or other symbol to let you know when it has been completed as it is meant to be.

That's why we use an outline. This is a dynamic, living document that bends and evolves and keeps us on track, while also allowing for creativity and a change of mind along the way. Without an outline we are adrift atop the Sargasso Sea; with it and we float effortlessly through the Atlantic side of the Strait of Gibraltar and into the Mediterranean Sea.

What follows here is the exact process I use with my clients as they begin their non-fiction book and complete it in a way that makes sense in terms of time, as related to level of productivity over a six to eight week period.

I begin by giving my book a tentative title and subtitle. This will typically change over the course of the time I am writing the book, especially the subtitle. I want it to as accurately as possible explain what the book is about.

Working Title:
Why am I writing this book?
What this book will be about:
Who will be served/target audience?

Precept: This is your Core Belief and Big Idea for your book.

My goal is to read everything I possibly can on this topic, from marketers, small business owners, and others dedicated to helping local businesses thrive. From this plethora of information, I will be able to draw my own conclusions and to better flesh out what I want to purposely include in my book and what I will intentionally exclude.

Books on this topic: Find at least six books on your topic and list them, along with the author and the year they were first published. Use the "Look Inside" feature on Amazon to see which topics are covered. Create an "Amazon List" to be able to access your choices more easily.

Keywords: Which words and phrases will people in your target audience use to find your book?

List of topics you will include in your book:
List of topics you will exclude from your book:
Websites on this topic:
Movers/Shakers/Thought Leaders in this niche:
Articles on this topic:

The Four Questions: These are based on the teachings of Simon Sinek

- What is? What is your topic?
- Why? Why is it important?
- What if? What if readers follow what you're sharing?
- How? How do you do what you are sharing?

And I've added another question. What's next? Additional content for your book

Now It's Time to Start Writing!

I like to begin by writing something for my Preface and Introduction. Then I write something for each of the sections. And then I dig into the first chapter to share my thoughts and ideas. If I get stuck, I always go back to my outline and see if I need to make some changes. For example, I may have too much content for one of my chapters or sections and need to rearrange. Or, something I thought I had much to write about in a specific chapter or section may not have as much as I thought. Once you have a tight outline you are able to write each day and your book comes together nicely. If you become lost at any point, go back to your outline and tighten it up.

Dedication (whom should I thank and/or acknowledge?)

Foreword: (Why the reader should read the book)

The foreword is the place for a guest author to show the reader why they should be reading this book. The foreword of a book is a major selling tool for the book. If it is written properly, and by the appropriate person for the job, the book's author will gain a lot of credibility in the reader's eyes. It is important to remember that the author of the book should not write the foreword.

Preface: (How the book came about) The preface is a place for the book's author to tell the reader how this book came into being, and why. It should build credibility for the author and the book. The preface is very similar to the foreword, except that the preface is written by the book's author. The preface is also an important selling tool for the book. Here the author should explain why they wrote the book, and how they came to write it. The author should be showing the reader why they are worth reading.

Introduction: (About the content of the book) The introduction introduces the material that is covered in the book. Here the author can set the stage for the reader and prepare them for what can be expected from reading the book. The introduction is a way for the author to grab the reader, and intensify the reader's desire to find out more, and hopefully devour the entire book. In the introduction, the author can quickly and simply tell the reader what is to be revealed in much greater detail if they continue reading.

Now it's time to start filling in your outline. For each section I will write one or two pages as an overview of what I will be sharing within the chapters in that section. For each chapter I will come up with three sub-topics that will be included within that chapter. For example, for my recent book on local business marketing this is what I had in my outline for the first section:

Section One - What is Marketing for Small Businesses?

Chapter One - *The History of Marketing*

    1) How businesses got the word out a century ago

    2) How Radio and Television Changed Marketing

    3) Marketing and Advertising Perceptions Based on Broadcasting

Chapter Two - Modern Day Marketing - Online and Offline

    1) Importance of Building Meaningful, Strategic Relationships

    2) Positioning Yourself as an Expert on Your Topic

    3) Networking Locally for Celebrity Status

Chapter Three - *Leveraging the Power of the Internet*
1) *Websites for Small Businesses*
2) *Virtual Storytelling*
3) *Email Marketing*

At the end of the book I have included:

Summary - What did I share in this book and how the reader can implement what they have learned by reading it

About the Author - Share as much information about yourself as is relevant to the reader and to your topic.

The outline is both the heart and the backbone of your book. It helps to center you as you choose what to include, as well as what to include within your pages. It also gives you strength to share your message with the people in the world who need to hear it, and to receive it only from you.

PART II

Turning Your Book Into a Business

"The first reason why I personally wanted to write a book is that books just last forever."

~ Jason Fladlien

Part II is about the strategy and technology of turning a book into a business.

In Chapter 4, I talk about the importance of relationships. This is crucial for authors because writing is generally a solitary process, but a business can't exist without others – customers and partners. This chapter also includes an interview with Jason Fladlien, a highly successful entrepreneur who wrote a book to grow his already-successful business.

Chapter 5, The Art and Science of the Funnel, explains the process of using your book to make a free offer to get subscribers so that you can sell them products and services. This chapter gets a little technical, but follow along, because you'll need to understand the basics of an online business.

Chapter 6 covers the many ways to create relationships via email.

Chapter 7 is about developing your business on your website and creating a selling platform for your products and services. I also cover 4 possible funnels that you'll want to consider.

In Chapter 8, I explain how to use social media to grow your business—and how to use social media strategically without wasting time.

CHAPTER 4

Importance of Relationships

"Trust is the glue of life. It's the most essential ingredient in effective communication. It's the foundational principle that holds all relationships."

~ Stephen Covey

You can't create a thriving business by yourself. You need to build relationships. Obviously, you need customers and clients, but they aren't enough.

You might be surprised by that statement, but the truth is that it's almost impossible to get enough customers and clients in your business just by your own efforts. You...

- won't reach enough people
- will have to work too hard to reach enough people
- will spend too much money reaching enough people

Relationships with others will help you get readers and buyers, but for this book, we're focusing on creating relationships with readers—people who have bought your book. When you do this properly, readers become customers.

Without creating a relationship with your customers, you'll struggle because while you might make some sales, the true gold is in repeat sales – and these require a relationship.

As an author, your words create a relationship with your reader. Readers feel like they get to know you through what you write. But to turn your book into a thriving business, you need more.

In this chapter, we'll talk about how to create the relationships that turn your book into a business.

Relationships Are the Start of Transformation

Readers want a transformational experience. They get that by applying what you teach (if you're writing non-fiction) or by the immersive nature of – or the message in -- what you write (especially if you write fiction).

They want to be changed or inspired by what they read. When you can create a transformational experience, you'll have readers asking for more! As a result, you have an opportunity to create a relationship with them – to offer them related products or books.

If you write non-fiction, you're more likely to offer related products or services. Examples are self-study courses and coaching. If you write fiction, you're more likely to offer additional books, whether yours or those of other similar authors. Either way, you can turn one purchase into additional purchases.

And the deeper and closer the relationship, the better the opportunity for a transformation – because one book might not be enough, right? To really change lives, you need some give and take with people. You need to find out exactly what they need and give it to them. You need to listen to them.

But how do you create relationships without dealing with all of your customers one-on-one? Doing that would involve so much of your time that you wouldn't be able to help many people at all!

The key is to create a structure of products and services that meet the needs of as many people in your target market, demographic or psychographic as possible. Some products will be low-cost and many people will be able to use them. Others will be more expensive but give people a more customized solution to their needs.

Let's talk more about how you can use the one-way relationship you create in your book into a more complex relationship that creates a money-making business.

The important thing to remember is when you continue the relationship you:

- Have more opportunities to help people
- Can create a business that starts with your book
- Can make more money

Relationships are Key to Creating a Money-Making Business from Your Book

When you sell your book, you don't automatically get a way to contact your reader, especially if the reader buys your book at a bookstore, on Amazon.com, etc. However, there ARE ways to sell a book and get immediately access to your reader. One way is to sell your book from your website. In that case, you get the buyer's name and email. Later in this book, we'll talk more about creating and maintaining relationships with email.

But if you're selling on Amazon, for example, you need to convince your reader to contact you. The most common way to do this is to have an offer at the beginning of the book – and you can repeat it several times throughout.

The offer is almost always for something free that is related to your book. It can be a report, worksheet, video, audio, template, checklist – anything that will help your reader get more value from your book.

In order to get that free offer (often called a freebie), your reader has to fill out a form, providing a name (usually just the first name) and a valid email address. The form contains code that you get from your email service provider and it stores the data so that you can subsequently send emails to the reader.

Note: Your email service provider also gives you the framework to send out multiple emails in compliance with spam, privacy, and other laws.

Without techniques for creating relationships with your readers, you are likely to lose track of them after they buy and read your book. But when you create a relationship, you can discover what they want, make them relevant offers, and grow your business.

Let's delve deeper into this process.

Opportunities and Techniques for Creating Relationships in an Online Business

So how do you create and develop meaningful relationships with many readers at one time? You develop something called a "funnel." In the next chapter, we'll go deeper into funnels, but for now, you should understand that a funnel draws the reader into a series of emails and then purchases.

Just as a real funnel starts large and has a small opening at the bottom, the number of readers and potentials readers may be large but a smaller number flow through to become your subscribers and then customers. However, without a funnel, there is almost no flow-through. You would only hear from the most fanatic readers who go out of their way to find you.

The funnel is the mechanism for you to create a relationship with your readers. You help them to get more out of your book while helping them to get to know you and what else you have to offer. The funnel is what lies between your book and a thriving business.

An Interview with Jason Fladlien

I (Ellen Finkelstein) interviewed Jason Fladlien for about 45 minutes about his book to business experience after reading his book, *One to Many*. You'll learn a lot about how to use a book to grow your business from him.

Here's a summary of what Jason has accomplished:

Jason Fladlien is known as the $100 million dollar webinar man. His pitch webinars have set records in the information, coaching, affiliate, and software space. Not only do many claim him to be the best webinar presenter out there, he is also considered the best teacher of webinars. He draws upon his eclectic background for inspiration, including being a Hare Krsna monk and a rapper born and raised in the small town of Muscatine, Iowa.

As such, people like Joe Polish describe him as "one of the top 5 living marketers on the planet." Jason enjoys his role as Chief Strategy Officer and co-founder of Rapid Crush, Inc., a company who has pioneered many different digital marketing methods that are considered standard today.

Due to his unrelenting passion for achievement, Jason has risen to the top of several industries including selling physical products on Amazon, as well as digital products, software, and coaching.

By having so much success in many different areas of business, Jason is often called in by 7, 8 and even 9-figure companies to help them with their marketing.

When he's not working, he's enjoying life with his beautiful wife and three children in Southern California. His hobbies include chess, music composition, listening to epic fantasy novels, and hiking with Bryce, his German Shepherd.

Here is a selection from the interview...

Ellen: Why did you write your book, One to Many?

Jason: The first reason is books just last forever. I have created over a hundred courses now in my life at various sizes and price points and they have a very short shelf life but the reality is pretty much the fabric of our existence revolves around books, if you really stop and think about it. As kids, hopefully we were read books to when we were tucked in at night. I've read hundreds of books to my kids at night. The whole concept of Western religion is built upon a singular book called the

Bible. We go to school and we learn from books for the most part even today with technology the way it is. Books are still the primary teaching tool and so people love books. I wanted to have something that would last longer than a digital course would, so that was one of the major reasons that I wrote it.

The second thing is that high-end clients read books. If I want to serve multimillionaires and billionaires, it's very hard to get them to consume courses cold. Millionaires and billionaires read a disproportionately high number of books compared to those who make less than a million dollars and a book is the ultimate portable thing that you can still reference and Kindle technology has made it even easier

You get this dual market that you can serve with a book that you normally can't serve anywhere else because a book is also the cheapest thing. I've spent 1/100 of the time on courses that we sell for $5,000 than I spent writing my book. It's funny that we would spend the most amount of time on something that we price these days the cheapest way. You can start a commerce relationship with our company, Rapid Crush, by buying the book. So, the easiest way to get a lead for the most part if you're in an information business is to sell them a book. At the same time, it's the best way to work with the high-end clients which we work a lot with. The idea is it's the most appealing thing, but it takes the most effort to create it.

In my case I wanted to write a "real book" – at 338 pages it was a massive undertaking – and treat it as if it's a book on the caliber of any book that you'd find in Barnes & Noble. This is not the only way to write a book, certainly not even the most recommended way, but for me and my point in time, in my place in my business, that's what I wanted to do. I knew it would be a way for us to get clients in the service business -- because we're more of a service orientated business these days -- so the book became the lead gen to get clients.

It's also a great way to get speaking engagements. It's a great way to have impact when I do podcasting. I've found the biggest leverage you can get if you're interviewed on the podcast is telling people to go buy your book on Amazon and that will get you more bang for your buck on the podcast than any other thing I've ever tried to market in any other way, shape or form. People trust a book just because they can they can see much more clearly that you know your stuff because it's so much more in-depth as compared to doing the webinar which is what your book is about.

So that's why I thought it was time in my career to write a book. It's definitely not the first place I would go if I was trying to start to make money online but once you've really developed a certain level of presence or you have other assets that you can leverage, a book is the perfect thing.

Ellen Finkelstein: How did you write the book? In other words, what was the process that you used to write the book?

Jason: First of all, I just set a goal to write one hour a day for 30 days straight. I felt if I wrote an hour a day for 30 days straight then I'd have enough material to have my book done. I wrote my book during the busiest time of the year. We were in the middle of a major product launch so I might have picked the worst time to start writing a book, but it didn't really matter -- if it was going to get done, it was going to get done.

So I would just wake up every day and write for an hour. Now the caveat to that every bit of information that went in the book was already in my head so I didn't have to do any research. That doesn't mean that you should only write books that are completely derivative of your experience -- certainly that's one way to do it -- but if you have to do research there's a lot more upfront work and effort and that's where an outline would become way more important.

I just basically wrote straight start to finish. I knew the process so well because I've taught it in so many other forms and media in person. I kind of just worked backwards from the fact that all that knowledge it was in my head and also the organization of it was all already in my head because I had taught it as a course. The way that I think about anything is sequentially or process orientated, so anything I do repeatedly ends up being broken down into a system. If you look at my webinars, I say in the introduction these five things must get accomplished and each thing has three to five ways to accomplish that, so there are 20 to 25 factors that I'm considering in my introduction. The content portion is the same way so it becomes really easy for me to teach it because I'm just literally teaching you the same logical sequential system that I use.

Here's what I did that I thought was most helpful and that I do all the time: I start with a blank sheet of paper and say, if I could teach anything and everything in time wasn't an option I could put in everything in this book possible what would I put into it and then I'll write down everything big or small. I don't censor myself and I come up with a list that is insane. I always say that subtraction is easier than addition. If you look at a lot of people with any project -- books courses --but any project they're trying to get done, people will want to prep their audience for every possible encounter but that's not helpful actually.

So I just say, let me get it all out of my system up front so that way it doesn't expand when I start to write it. Instead let me get everything and then let me cross everything out that's not needed so the essential is left. I'm a firm practitioner of the 80/20 rule, which is that a few things make a majority of the results. A few key teaching points are going to give the majority of value and so when it's done, I only have a few very tightly focused pieces of content that I have to cover.

Then you can expand on those. So you start with a lot, you subtract it down, and then what's left you expand on again. You've brought it down but then you develop those points but it's very structured already. I spend a lot of time on the few things that matter, not on a lot of stuff that doesn't matter. So, in One to Many, I explain that there are four elements to a webinar presentation. There's an intro, content, transition, and pitch, that's it. So I just teach you those four elements. There are a million other things that can matter but they matter a little bit. What really matters is these four things and then how you get people to your webinar and where you send them once they go to your webinar, that's it. It's really simplistic at the end of the day.

Before the book was finished, I took the book manuscript and created a 2-day live training and we sold that for $5,000 and it was functionally no different than what's in this book. From that we took the recordings, added some bonuses, dressed it up and now we sell the product called Genius Webinars which again is not that different from this book. All the content is originally derived from this manuscript but speaking it, teaching it, and showing additional examples of it -- that's where a few people will pay a lot of money because if a millionaire can get 1% better, our webinars can make them a million dollars. So, they read the book to see he knows what he's talking about but if they want to hear him use this technique or do this thing or that thing they will happily pay more for less information but more tightly focused.

So the great thing is I knew going in that I would be able to use this material in other fashions beyond just the book so that's what made me really discipline myself to really capture it in its perfect format in the book -- so I could derive from it in perpetuity.

Ellen Finkelstein: Did you outsource anything?

Jason: I did outsource the layout, the typography and the design. I used a company called Scribe Media. They also write books for authors from start to finish. They are super high-end so I think I paid like $20 grand, but it was important to me. They took care of the Kindle version for me, too, and they did a lot of the little things that for most authors do not matter but my goal was to look just as professional and as high-quality from the paper to the font as you would see with a major publisher.

Now most people don't have to do any of that -- you could simply take it to Fiverr and you could upload it through Amazon itself and you'll probably get 80% of the way there and it's going to be good enough. But for me because on the back of this we're selling $30 thousand services upfront with a continuity of $2,000 a month it made sense for us to invest in that. And then copy editing was a major part of it as well because I wanted it to read like a professional company edited it because if you read really highly qualified published books from major publishers, they have incredibly good copy editors. But again that does not really matter to most people and it shouldn't necessarily be the thing that you should worry about if you're writing a book but for us at the stage of the career that we were at and the profile that we had and all the ways I knew that this thing was going to make me money, it was okay for me to splurge. But I wrote every word of the book myself.

Again, I don't think it matters for most people. Here's the thing that I learned in this -- I would rather get it to market and be good enough and then see if I can sell it because if I can't sell it or distribute it give it away for free then it doesn't matter how good it is. If I can distribute it, then I should go back and update it for Version two and then I can do all the things that I wanted to do that don't really matter too much on Version one.

Ellen Finkelstein: How did you use the book to grow your business?

Jason: There are a ton of ways that you can use it so whenever I speak at a conference, we either have the organizer buy books and distribute them to everybody or if we think it's important enough, we will personally bring the books and distribute them ourselves to every single client. Within the book there are calls to actions to go opt-in to get some additional thing which puts them on our email list and we can follow up. There are also direct calls to action at the end of the book if they wanted to hire our company to create the webinars for them so that's one of the ways that we use it.

Another way that we use it is obviously if I'm getting interviewed on the podcast, my call to action now is to go buy the book on Amazon because people listening to a podcast can one click purchase on Amazon right on their phone while they're listening to it so I've just found that that's super effective.

The call to action within the book so that they can get on our email list is the major thing – there are strategic calls to action that have extra bonuses and supplemental content so once they book then they go to a place and then that place opts them in.

You know it's so crazy and surreal for me to think about this but last week I think... You know we're on the platform Zoom right now and so Zoom went public last week at $16 billion. So Zoom brought us in a few months ago to do training to their user base on how to use webinars and that was pretty nice. They gave us a real big push and we got a lot of people from Zoom themselves this has this worked out incredibly well.

At the beginning of the webinar I said, "I'm going to talk to you about how to use webinars. You know the most important part about a webinar at the end of the day is the presentation but I'm not going to dive into the ins and outs of a presentation today. I'm going to mostly focus on how you promote the webinar and what types of webinars you should use, but because the presentation is so important, I wrote a whole book on this and you can buy it if you go to Amazon but I'll make you a deal. If you go to rapidcrush.com/zoom you can download it for free for a limited time." There were four or five times on this hour-long training when I did a call to action to get the book for free so people on the webinar were sent to a special page where they can opt in to download the PDF version of this book for free and then on the thank you page we say if you'd like to have us talk to you to see if we can help you implement or best use webinars, book a time in the calendar. So we ended up with, I think, 70 appointments from the small time that we did with Zoom.

So we helped Zoom by being of value, teaching their users to better use their platform therefore being more valuable users to Zoom and in exchange for that Zoom sent us leads that we can then service ourselves. If we service those leads, guess what, they're going to use Zoom even more, so it's a very synergistic relationship. Corporate clients and bigger enterprise value type of clients are all comfortable promoting a book or allowing you to utilize a book where they're not as comfortable have you sell anything on that webinar. They're totally OK with you promoting a book even though we had attendees opt in and we built a huge list from that and then we sold our services on the back end. That didn't bother them because we led with the book and we gave it away for free. Now we're talking about doing even more business with them and then we can take that model and we have apply it in many other places as well.

So the book is super powerful if you're doing any virtual presentations for audiences where you can't sell or don't want to sell because you're uncomfortable or don't have anything else to sell.

Ellen Finkelstein: That was one of my questions about giving it away for free.

Jason: We don't usually give the book away because we know if people don't pay for it they're very unlikely to actually read it so that's just a consideration that we have because we have other authority that is super credible that we leverage instead.

Ellen Finkelstein: You talked a little bit about that the calls to action in the books. Could you want to go in more than detail because we talked a lot about that in our course.

Jason: That's probably one of the most important things you can do in your book. I will tell you the things that have the biggest leverage in the short term and then the biggest leverage in the long term.

Having an incredibly well-written book in the long term is a huge advantage but in the short term it is very minimal. It's only an advantage after five years believe it or not. It's very hard to get people to read your full book and then if they read it, to get them to be excited about it and tell other people about it. But then you look at some of my favorite books, they took 10 to 20 years to become bestsellers because they were so good they were undeniable, so people would tell their friends and then they would tell them again and then tell him a fifth time and then by the fifth time that person decided they were going to buy the book.

There are a lot of average books are on the New York Times bestseller list so in the short term what really matters from your book are a couple things -- the first thing is the title of your book. More than anything in the short term, your title is going to be your biggest leverage point. If I had a hundred hours to write a book and I really wanted it to be successful I'd spend 50 hours on the title alone. The title is the headline, that's how powerful the title is from a marketing perspective. So you should always be thinking about titles even when you're not writing books because eventually you're going to stumble upon a title that just completely electrifies.

The second most important thing is the Foreword, who's writing your Foreword. In the long term, you could have a really bad title and you probably do okay. In the long term, you don't need a Foreword at all and you're probably okay but in the short term a really good title with a Foreword by somebody who's famous or influential or powerful within your market or somebody that's well-known, that's super leverageable.

So I had Joe Polish write my Foreword. Most people in the business world consider Joe the most connected, networked guy in business and in the Foreword Joe says I'm one of the top-5 marketers alive in his estimation and so for a lot of audiences that carries a lot of weight and that's very, very powerful.

Then the next most important thing on equal footing with the book itself is how you're going to get somebody from the book to take additional action and that's the call to action in the call-outs. So it's twofold -- it's what do you say in the book to get them to go outside of the book and opt in, send a text message, or do something so you can then put them into your universe beyond just the book. So how do you phrase that and how do you position that?

One of the things that I did that was unique-ish was make the calls to action stand out. Anytime you see those gray "Johnson boxes," those are usually calls to action although not always. So we mixed them so usually they were calls to action, but sometimes they weren't in a box.

We also wrote unique calls to action so that they weren't always the same copy and put one before Page one. It says, "Get your free webinar goodies and bonuses at http://webinarextras.com." That domain name is easy to remember and to type in so just giving it its own domain and putting it right away at the very beginning makes it very, very soft. Then as it goes on you can get a little bit more forceful if you wish, although I don't recommend that.

And then I just displayed one more, at the end of most chapters. I would write something like, "I put together several resources to assist you with getting the most of this book. To access these resources go to..." and then there's the call to action.

Sometimes I will find actual content so I'll be quoting one of our webinars like a transcript and then say, "Hey, would you like to this listen to me do this? It's over here." And then I'll say, "Hey, these slide designs — would you like to download my template? Go here." or "Here's the funnel."

We had a whole bunch of different resources. The last chapter is basically a sales letter so it's hard-hitting and it tells you what to do.

Really what matters is its own unique domain separate from everything else that's ideally short and easy to type with a lot of different goodies that are enticing but not selling them a whole bunch of stuff. You always have to sell even if it's free. They have to give you their information but it's not overwhelming. With a whole bunch of resources you can pair and match them with the content.

If you don't have that, if you have one simple thing like "what we're doing for clients now," you can say, "Would you like the free web class companion to this book? Go here" and then say, "Hey this point was so important, it's one of the key points we talk about in the free web class, so go here" and that's your call-to-action. So now you just build a webinar that highlights the most important parts in the book and then they can go there and watch that webinar.

So use multiple calls to action in strategic locations that are very easy to act upon.

I think for a lot of markets the easiest way these days is text messages. For example, "text webinars to phone number" and then from there you can send them a link. What's most important is having multiple calls to action spread throughout.

Ellen Finkelstein: This was fun! It was really valuable and will be helpful for authors. You did say you were going to tell me something about millionaires and billionaires and how you were reaching them.

Jason: They're the same concept of what we did with Zoom. If we can get them the book and then use the book to get our foot in the door, that's the most effective thing I've ever found, because a billionaire will read a book on a private flight, they will read it on their device and it's finding a way for them to not just get the book but then read the book. It's spending all that money on making it read well and look good and all that kind of stuff so it's impressive, yes it matters for those audiences. For most people, they just want to know, is it good or not? The content if it could be written on a piece of toilet paper but if it's powerful, they don't care. But when you get to the big leagues, this creates a trust factor.

Ellen Finkelstein: Thanks so much!

Jason: All right, thank you, bye-bye.

CHAPTER 5

The Art and Science of the Funnel

"Sometimes we make the process more complicated than we need to. We will never make a journey of a thousand miles by fretting about how long it will take or how hard it will be. We make the journey by taking each day step by step and then repeating it again and again until we reach our destination."

~ *Joseph B. Wirthlin*

In this chapter, we'll discuss the funnel in more detail and show you how you can use it to turn your book into a business. While creating a funnel involves some technology, it isn't difficult, and the processes and concepts are fairly simple.

What is a Funnel?

A funnel is a series of offers.

In the last chapter, we talked about offering something for free inside your book. That's the first offer and it sends the reader to a webpage that you own or control with an opt-in form (sometimes called a sign-up form). As we mentioned earlier, you get the code for the form from your email service provider.

Connie uses Aweber (http://ConnieLoves.me/Aweber) and Ellen uses BirdSend (https://EllenHelps.me/birdsend). This makes creating the opt-in form a fairly simple copy and paste operation. You don't need to understand the code!

The opt-in form serves two important purposes:
- It stores the reader's name and email address in your account with your email service provider
- When the form is completed, it gives you permission to email the reader

So, you can now set up a system for contacting the reader. You can make further offers in those emails. Later in this book, we'll talk more about how this system works.

Finally, you can make offers on a web page. Readers can get to that web page through a link in an email, after completing the opt-in form, or from a link on social media.

To summarize, you can place offers that are part of your funnel in three places:

- In your book (digital or print) or another product
- In emails
- On your website

Types of Offers You Should Make

Which types of offers should you make? Should you promote a product, a free offer, a course, a strategy session, or something else?

In almost all cases, you want to promote a free offer that's related to the book. The reason for this is that you want to start by getting your readers' email addresses and the highest chance of doing that is with something for free.

The free offer should have real value and help people with the same problem that your book solves. It can be a supplement to the book, such as a workbook or checklist that helps readers implement the content of the book. You might invite readers to join your Facebook group if you can make the case that this is valuable enough.

If you're writing fiction, you could create a short guide to the back story of the main characters or a pamphlet telling your own story and how it led to the book.

- **Related products:** Your products, Private Label Rights products, affiliate products (we'll explain these later in this book)

- **Related services:** Done-for-you services, an assessment, coaching
- **Memberships:** Offering a trial month of a membership at a low price is a great way to get recurring income

Your offer should make clear that subscribers will get emails—give them a clue as to the content and frequency. This provides the transparency that is required by the General Data Protection Regulation (GDPR), a European Union law that requires transparency and privacy. You can put a short statement to this effect below the opt-in form.

Later in this chapter, I'll explain how you can use offers without an opt-in form.

How to Add an Offer in Your Book

Let's start by talking about your first offer, the one in your book. (Actually, you can make offers of bonuses to potential book buyers on your website, as part of your launch, but that's a different topic.)

How do you add an offer in your book? It's simple—you add a link that goes to a web page you own or control. Be sure to consider your book's format and the convenience of your reader when you do this. Here are some guidelines:

- If your book will be electronic – a PDF ebook or a Kindle – you can make an electronic link that people can click or tap. But people may not want to fill out a form on their phone or tablet, so you should ALSO write out the link so people can type it in.
- If your book will be printed, you need to write out the link so people can type it in.
- For a printed book, you can use a QR code, which is an image that people can scan with a QR reader (generally with a phone app). Once scanned, the person is taken to the

desired web page. Note that many people don't have a QR reader, so you shouldn't depend on a QR code alone.

- Keep your links short so people can easily type them. Either create short page names or use a link shortener like bit.ly.

Pay attention to the web page you're linking to because you want as many people as possible who get there to complete the form. The percentage of visitors to that page who actually sign up is called the "conversion rate" because you're converting visitors (readers) to subscribers. The page should be:

- Very relevant to the topic of the book and to your readers
- As irresistible (valuable) as possible
- Attractive—use a big image!
- Easy to read
- Simple so that people can skim and get right to the opt-in form

Where to Add Offers in Your Book

Where should you put your book's offer? Well, first of all, you should put it in more than one place. And yes, you can have more than one type of offer in different places, but focus on one main offer. Remember that your main goal is to turn readers into subscribers.

Why should you put the offer in several places? There are several reasons for this.

1) On Amazon, browsers can click the "Look Inside" button to see the first few pages of your book and if one of those pages has a free offer, you can get subscribers even if people don't buy your book!

2) While you certainly wrote your book to be useful throughout, you'd be surprised how many people don't finish a book that they buy. If you leave your offer to the end, many people will never see it.

3) Readers may need to see an offer several times before they decide to take you up on it. Once you have engaged them and they start to understand your content and appreciate your expertise, they'll be more amenable to giving you their name and email address.

How Many Offers Should You Have?

However, different people might be interested in different offers and as you cover a variety of topics in your book, you might find that a variety of offers in your chapters gets you more subscribers. In this situation, you'll have multiple opt-in forms on multiple web pages that you link to, each sending people to a different list or tag in your email service provider's system.

For example, let's say you're writing a book about losing weight. In the book, you might cover both diet and exercise. Some people will be more interested in diet and others in exercise. So you could have two free offers:
1) Daily Food Tracking Form
2) Daily Exercise Tracking Form

In this way, you can attract more readers based on which is most interesting to them.

Offers without an Opt-In Form

Your readers are more likely to complete an opt-in form if they know you a little bit and what better way to help them get to know you but with a video of you speaking about your topic?

Tamara Monosoff (www.tamaramonosoff.com) is an expert in this topic and she recommends that you record a short video (1-3 minutes) for each chapter. You link to this video at the beginning of each chapter. In the video, you tell people what value they'll get from the chapter. That video is on a page on your website, where you can again make your free offer if you want. But the offer in the book is just for the free video.

If your videos are engaging enough, people will continue to watch them and hopefully by the end of the book, they'll opt in. You can even ask them to do so in the video.

CHAPTER 6

Continuing Your Relationships Via Email

Relationships feed on credibility, honesty, and consistency.

~Scott Borchetta

Let's say that some of your readers opt-in and are now listed as subscribers in your email service provider. What now? You can't email them individually, so you need to set up an automated system. Luckily, email service providers have the tools you need.

The purpose of the emails is to create a relationship with your subscribers so that you can turn them into customers. Never forget that. Let's start with setting up the system and then we'll explain how to use emails to turn readers into buyers.

Setting Up Your Email System

There are many email service providers (ESPs) and of course, some are better than others. You don't need a fancy, expensive one, but you do need one that will make it easy for you to create that relationship with your readers.

Choosing the right email service provider is important. Features to consider are:

- Reliability and deliverability rate
- Service (if you are technically challenged, pay a little extra for phone support)
- Automation features, such as tagging and autoresponders
- Flexibility, so you can choose what happens when a person completes an opt-in form

All modern email service providers have 4 features and you need to understand these well. If you are already familiar with an email service provider, you can skip this section. On the other hand, we've seen that some authors are using older providers or are not using all available features, so you might discover something new!

Subscriber list

As we've been describing, when your readers complete an opt-in form, they end up in a database in your email service provider. While we've mentioned that you generally collect a first name and email address, a database can include more information than that. For example, maybe in your business it's advantageous to collect telephone numbers. On the other hand, the more information you ask for, the less likely people will complete the form. So you need to consider carefully what information to request.

The subscriber list can be segmented in several ways. Each offer you have should go to a different segment. Older email service providers use the concept of lists, so that each opt-in form puts subscribers into a different list. Newer ones use the concept of tags, so that each opt-in form assigns a different tag to the subscriber. Some ESPs use both systems. The tag method is more flexible because people can have multiple tags, but either system can work for you. (Subscribers can be on multiple lists, but some ESPs count each instance of a subscriber when they charge you.)

Why is segmenting important? Segmenting lets you send out emails that are appropriate to the interests of your subscribers. To follow the earlier example of people interested in diet vs. exercise, you might want to send different emails to the two groups of people, focusing on their chosen interest.

Broadcast emails

Of course, all ESPs let you send out "broadcast" emails, which are emails that you choose to send whenever you want. These are not sent automatically, but whenever you decide to email your subscribers. You use broadcast emails for the long-term relationship with your subscribers and to build your business.

We'll discuss broadcast emails a bit later in this chapter.

Opt-in forms

We've already mentioned that ESPs give you the code for opt-in forms. Here's the general process for creating an opt-in form, although the details vary with the ESP:

1) You create a new opt-in (or sign-up) form. You set the fields (usually first name and email address) that you want to collect.
2) You specify which list or tag subscribers are assigned to.
3) You may design the form, including colors, title, etc. If you're using a page builder in WordPress or have a web designer designing your website, the design may be done on your website rather than in your ESP.
4) You copy the code that the ESP gives you. You may have a choice of JavaScript and HTML code and can try each one to see which works best.
5) You open the page where you want the form to go and display the view where you can put code. In WordPress, this is on the Text tab/mode rather than the Visual tab/ mode.
6) You paste the code where you want it to go.

This isn't very hard and your ESP's support can walk you through it.

Autoresponders/automation

Autoresponders are just what they sound like – emails that are sent automatically. They are very powerful in their ability to create relationships with new subscribers, yet many authors do not use them well – if at all!

Setting up autoresponders is different in different ESPs. You'll usually find the settings under a special autoresponder section—autoresponders may be called automation, campaigns, drips, sequences, or something else. There will be a place to create the series of emails that you want new subscribers to get, specify how long to wait between emails (such as a day), and perhaps assign a tag when the autoresponder series is done. Assigning a tag when the autoresponder series is done is important to avoid sending your regular broadcasts to people who are new subscribers and are still getting your initial autoresponders. If you send out a lot of broadcasts, this can be a little overwhelming to new subscribers.

You'll assign the autoresponder series to an opt-in form, so that when people complete the form, the autoresponder series starts automatically.

Those four components of an ESP – subscriber list, broadcast emails, opt-in forms, and autoresponders – are all you need to understand to start turning your readers into customers.

Using Autoresponders to Continue the Funnel

Autoresponders are key to creating valuable relationships with new subscribers and moving them through the funnel. The open rate of autoresponders is very high, much higher than of broadcast emails. That's because the level of interest of new subscribers is very high at the beginning of the relationship.

Here's an example of how you can use autoresponders to create a relationship with new subscribers:
1) Subscribers complete your opt-in form.
2) Subscribers automatically see a "thank-you" page which tells them to watch for an email with the information they requested. If you want, you can put a paid offer on this page—or a video.

3) Subscribers get an email (the first autoresponder) with a link to a web page (the "delivery" page)
4) Subscribers click the link in the email to go to the web page where they can click the link to get the free offer
5) The next day, another autoresponder arrives, asking subscribers if they have any questions and inviting them to reply to you.
6) The following day, another autoresponder arrives with a couple of tips to help them get more out of the free offer (and your book) and maybe a link to a video of you talking about your topic.
7) The day after that, another autoresponder arrives with a discount on a related offer.

These autoresponders can go on – it's not uncommon to have 7-15 of them.

Can you see how autoresponders accomplish four things? Here they are:

1) They deliver the promised free offer
2) They create a relationship by linking to a video and asking subscribers to reply to you
3) They help subscribers get more out of the offer – and your book
4) They make an offer for a product

You can't accomplish all of this without autoresponders!

Using Broadcast Emails for Relationship Building

The other side of ESPs is broadcast emails. As we said, these are emails that you choose to send out at any time to your subscribers and you use them for long-term relationships. Your emails can contain many types of content, but here are some examples:

- **Tips on the topic of your book:** For example, Ellen has a Daily Hot Tip related to Internet Marketing and succeeding with an online business.
- **A link to your latest blog post:** Your blog is a way for you to show off your expertise on your topic and expand on your book. Your subscribers are interested in this topic, so you should continue to offer them more content. Each blog post should end with a call to action – this can be as simple as asking people to comment or you can make a free or paid offer.
- **Offers for your products or those of others (which would use an affiliate link so you can get a commission):** Authors often shy away from selling, but if you want a business, you need to make offers!
- **Free offers:** These can be yours or those of others (using an affiliate link so you get a commission)
- **Stories:** You're an author, so you know how to tell stories! Readers want to hear about you and what you're doing. They also appreciate stories about others that offer relevant messages.

As long as you regularly make a variety of offers, you'll be able to make money. They key word here is "variety." You can't offer the same one product over and over to the same people. In the end, you'll probably add on a combination of affiliate marketing (promoting products of others) and creating products with rebrandable content that you purchase (Private Label Rights content).

CHAPTER 7

Developing Your Business on Your Website

Email is only one place where you can create relationships and move new subscribers through your funnel so that they become customers. Email is important because it's where you start the relationship—remember that you put a link in your book to an opt-in page and readers fill out the form to get your free offer. They get that free offer via email.

But perhaps the most obvious place to develop your business is on your website—or a third-party platform. When you're ready to sell, you need a way to accept credit cards and deliver your products or services.

Choosing the Right Selling Platform for Your Business

In order to have a business, you need to be able to sell products from your website or a third-party platform. Before we go into specific options, let's talk about the difference between using your website or a third-party platform. There are also blended options that use both your website and a third-party platform —in fact, these are very common. Let's discuss these options because there are advantages and disadvantages to each.

Selling from your website gives you most control and may be less expensive, depending on your selling platform. It also looks professional to sell directly from your website. But the more control you have, the more responsibility you have and you may find that the technical requirements are too much for you. Of course, you can outsource these tasks.

Getting a merchant account and gateway

You need both a merchant account (to hold the money you make) and a gateway (to process credit cards) but in most cases, you'll get these as a package. The 3 most popular are:

- **PayPal:** This is a merchant account and gateway combination. You'll need a business account. PayPal Payments Standard is easiest but moves buyers to PayPal's website during payment. PayPal Payments Pro requires more technical expertise but keeps buyers on your website. (There's also a monthly charge.) Get more information by visiting the link here. (https://www.paypal.com/us/webapps/mpp/payment-methods) We recommend PayPal for beginners.
- **Stripe:** This is similar to PayPal but may be a little harder for beginners. Stripe is known for great security. Get more information by visiting the link here. (https://stripe.com/US/payments)
- **Authorize.net:** This is a gateway but you can get it bundled with a merchant account that it recommends or use your own.

Choosing a shopping cart

You also need a shopping cart to create a "Buy" button on your website. Actually, you can, for example, use a simple PayPal Buy button but your options after that are limited. A shopping cart does several things:

1) Stores product information and displays it to your potential customer
2) Connects with your gateway and merchant account to process the payment
3) Informs you of the sale
4) Connects with your email service provider so you can send your customer an email with product information
5) Redirects buyers to a page of your choice so your customer can download an electronic product

Consider what you need. Do you want to offer recurring products, like a membership program? Do you want to drip content out over time? If you are using a WordPress website, are you OK with using a plug-in that you have to configure and update? Do you want 24/7 phone support? These are all issues that will help determine which solution you choose.

We won't go into great detail here, but here are some solutions for selling from your website:

- A simple PayPal button will give you the fewest options but it's the easiest solution for getting started quickly
- Many people use WooCommerce, a free WordPress plug-in. It has many paid add-ons if you need them.
- Some online options are <u>Zaxaa</u> (<u>https://EllenHelps.me/Zaxaa</u>), <u>Nanacast</u> (<u>http://ConnieLoves.me/Nanacast</u>), and 1ShoppingCart.
- Then there are third-party platforms that don't even require you to have a website, such as JVZoo, WarriorPlus, ClickFunnels, and LeadPages.

Here are considerations for making the right choice:

- Stability, security, and regularly updated
- Support
- East of use
- Cost
- Features – see the next sections in this chapter for some of the features you might look for

Creating Funnels for Your Business

Once you have the sales infrastructure in place, you need to create your funnels. Unless you use one of the third-party platforms, you'll create your funnels on your website. Either way, you can create simple or complex funnels. Start with simple ones until:

- You see what works for your audience
- You learn the process

It's very important to put yourself in your reader's shoes and think of all the possible entry points into your funnel. For example, someone who hasn't read your book may come to a blog post on your website and opt in for your freebie. On the other hand, someone who is reading your book may see your offer for your freebie and opt-in having already read your book. Do you see how you have to allow for people to come from various places and move them through the funnel in a meaningful way?

We've already discussed the 3 places to put offers – your book, your emails, and your website. And in the next chapter, we'll explain how creating a course based on your book is the natural next step in your funnel. And we've explained the technology of creating an opt-in form and a sales button. With all of that clear, let's look at some possible funnels that will turn your book into a thriving business.

1) **Book to freebie to course:** This is the most obvious funnel for authors who want to create a business from their book. In your book, you make an offer to a freebie with a link to the opt-in page. Then, in the freebie, you make an offer for a course based on the book.

2) **Email to freebie to book to course:** This assumes that you send an email to your subscribers offering them a freebie (which you might derive from your book). In the freebie, you make an offer for your book. In the book, you make an offer for the related course.

3) **Blog post to freebie to book to course:** This is like the previous funnel except that you write a blog post and promote it. Some people might find it by searching, too. In the blog post, you promote your freebie. In the freebie, you make an offer for your book. In the book, you make an offer for the related course. Or, you could promote your book in your blog post and from there, funnel #1 would work.

4) **Email to book to course:** In this funnel, you promote your book in an email. From there, people can find your freebie or your course.

The first contact can come from anywhere – joint venture partners, organic search on the Internet, ads, social media posts, and, of course, email.

Do you see that because you don't know where everyone will start, you need to make offers everywhere? So your book should include an offer for both your freebie and your course. Either way, readers will end up on your email list so you can make further offers and expand your business.

More about Funnels-Bumps, Upsells, and Downsells

Funnels can get sophisticated. When a person subscribes for your freebie, make an offer for your book or course on the thank-you/download page.

A sales funnel can include bumps, upsells, and downsells. In order to create these, your selling platform needs to offer them as a feature. These are somewhat advanced, so first get your main funnels working before trying these. Here are some helpful definitions:

- **Bump:** This is like "Do you want fries with that?" On the sales page, BEFORE a person clicks the Buy button, there's a checkbox that adds a low-priced addition. For example, you might add templates when a person buys a book from you.
- **Upsell:** Upsells comes AFTER the purchase. Before people get access to the product, they see another sales page that adds to the original product. They either click the Buy button or choose "No thanks."
- **Downsell:** Downsells also come AFTER the purchase and happen when a person chooses "No thanks" for an upsell or simply abandons a sales page or sales cart page. The downsell will be lower in price than the upsell or original product.

CHAPTER 8

Using Social Media to Grow Your Business

Social media platforms offer you many opportunities for promoting your book and your business. You can reach many people without cost, although you can reach more people if you buy ads. Here are some pointers for using social media effectively.

Creating Relationships on Social Media

In order for you to succeed in promoting your book and your business on social media, you need to be social! That means you need to systematically increase the number of your friends, contacts, and followers.

While you can – and should – automate posting on social media, you also need to be there in person for the personal touch. This means responding to comments on your posts and liking the posts of others.

Using Social Media Strategically

Social media can take you "down the rabbit hole" so be careful to use it strategically. Don't socialize for the sake of socializing. Get in, create a post, and get out. Look at your notifications and don't spend much time at all on your timeline or main feed.

Groups are also extremely valuable because they are organized around an interest. Join groups that contain people in your target market and post in them. Just be sure to follow the rules that are posted.

Making Offers on Social Media

Because social media is supposed to be social, you shouldn't just make offers all the time. Instead, you need to balance your posts with:

- Free information, including your blog posts, posts and articles of others, etc.
- Inspirational content to help others
- Your offers

When you find someone who seems to need your help, it's usually best to do a private message so that the conversation is personal. You can create some valuable relationships this way with not only potential customers but potential partners.

PART III

Creating an Online Course

What is an Online Course?

Another way to turn your book into a viable business and income stream is by creating online courses. I am defining an online course to be a training that is delivered on the internet and is digital in nature. This may be done through webinars, teleseminars, PDFs, or audio recordings. The student may receive this training through one of the methods I just mentioned or through multiple ones throughout the course.

Your online course may be found by your prospect through an email message, a social media update, a blog post, or through someone who is recommending it through an affiliate link.

They are then taken to a sales page, also located online where they are able to read every detail of what is being offered, and in what format, and at what cost. The online course may then be purchased on the internet and the new student is then taken to the web page or membership site where the content is available for them to download, and in some cases to sign up for future trainings that are also included.

As an author using your content to create your online course you may be thrilled to find out that you will now have the potential to make sales 24/7/365. Once you have delivered the live or pre-recorded training you will be able to earn ongoing income for as long as you wish, making updates when necessary and increasing the price when you add additional content.

Think back to a time when you purchased a DVD, CD, or book, most likely at a book store or other retailer. Understand these are all examples of the original content creator being able to deliver their writing or music or any other type of creative product to you after they have created this content for the first time.

In order to deliver with impact, not to mention expound at length on a subject, non-fiction books generally focus more on the book's reason for existence: It's "Why." Books help you understand all the ins and outs of a topic.

Courses are created to teach you "How." You need to discard any content that stops moving the "how to" process forward.

This is why even the most esoteric book can easily be converted into an online course that not only gets people from Point A to Point B but also shows them how to achieve a valuable result in the process. They want something tangible that has the potential to become life changing for them.

This may be an oversimplification, but understanding that basic principle will make converting any non-fiction book into an online course format much easier.

The best time to decide to create a course from your book material is when you are still in the planning stages for your book, unless your book is already completed. You can deliberately plan to elaborate or demonstrate certain chapters or topics and make sure your interviews, notes and material is gathered with this in mind. But even if your book is already out, creating a course from its contents and premise can be highly effective and profitable.

If your book has already been published for a year or longer, this is an excellent way to breathe life into it once again. You may even use your book as a bonus when someone signs up for your course. I've done this twice and this was an excellent way for me to request and receive more reviews and sales in a short period of time, pushing my book higher in the rankings.

CHAPTER 9

Importance of Having Your Own Online Course

I believe that we, as authors must create an online course to teach and supplement the information we have included in our book. To achieve success with this goal there are three tips I will share with you.

First, give your course the name your ideal student will find irresistible. Include the topic of your book, but change it slightly so it will be attractive to both your readers and prospects. Action verbs work well, as I discovered in my *Write. Publish. Prosper.* book, online course, and live event of the same name.

Then promise and demonstrate an extra level of depth and value that competing courses do not offer. I like to imagine myself teaching my students in a face-to-face setting where we are able to interact closely during the time we have together, and meeting for coffee or lunch months or years later as they have implemented and benefitted from what they learned from me.

Finally, break your course down into easily consumable chunks for better understanding and comprehension. The "fire hose" approach is never a good one. Instead, you will dole out your knowledge, experience, and expertise in a logical way, naturally moving your forward in a way that will transform their lives.

Before creating your online course, go through your book and pull out key points and concepts for slide creation. This will give you an excellent outline to build your course upon.

There's also one thing you need to do before you go any further; take at least one online course, if you haven't done so already to see how it's done and what it is like to be a student in this type of learning environment.

The "Know, Like, and Trust" Factor in Action

You will discover that the fastest path to massive visibility and enhanced credibility will be through creating and selling your online course. This is how it works:

Leveraging the power of the internet through your email list and with social media (both topics covered in detail by Ellen earlier in this book) you can be seen everywhere at once. You will also share your own story (also covered by Ellen in the next section) so that the world will know more about who you are and what you have to offer. This type of visibility is the "know and like" part of the equation.

When you launch your first online course you add in the "trust" piece by allowing people to learn from you personally within a small group setting. All of this is based on your being a published author, something that is considered a great achievement in all parts of the world.

I cannot overemphasize the power of creating an online course as a part of your overall marketing plan. Creating and selling your online course based on the content of your book will quickly set you apart from other authors and other entrepreneurs everywhere.

CHAPTER 10

Creating an Online Course

Now it is time to create your online course. Let's break this process down into some logical steps.

1) What Problem Are You Solving?
2) What Does the Goal Look Like?
3) Brain Dump Your Ideas
4) Organize Your Content
5) Create a Timeline
6) Outline Your Lessons
7) Separate Your Ideas and Content Into Modules
8) Write Your Lessons
9) Review What You Have Created
    9) (A) Bonus Materials
10) Delivering Your Online Course

What Problem Are You Solving?

As authors and authorpreneurs (authors who embrace the concept of entrepreneurship) we are in the business of problem solving. Your original idea that finally became your published book answered questions and solved problems for your reader. Your online course will do the same, and now you will have the opportunity to be interactive with the people who are served with your message and insight into your specific topic.

Imagine having the ability to get close enough to the author of a book that changed or transformed your life even in a small way. This is how your participants will feel when they have the opportunity to work with you within the virtual walls of your online course.

What Does the Goal Look Like?

When you think about the people who will connect with and learn from you by reading your book and going through your course, what does your "Big Picture" goal look like? Envision the person who will take this journey with you. What would they take away from your information? How will they be transformed? What would you like them to do next?

Give this as much thought as possible as you work your way through the process of creating your online course. Your goal is to serve the people who show up to work with you and you will want to make sure they get as much from the experience as they possibly can.

Brain Dump Your Ideas

This step is about getting all your thoughts and ideas about your topic out of your head. We all talk to ourselves throughout each day, and more than likely you have an ongoing conversation going on in your head about what you know and have already shared in your book.

You know so much about your topic, maybe even more than you realize. The problem is taking the information you know and putting it into something logical and coherent.

Most people don't go from ideas in their head to something amazing on paper; creating content is not a one-step process. The first phase of developing your content is to simply take it out of your head so you can see what you've already got.

This is similar to cleaning out your closet. You don't automatically know what you are going to keep and what you will donate. First, you have to see what clothes you have. Then you can decide what you are going to do with them.

It's the same for your course content. This is why you'll start developing your course content by doing a brain dump.

Brain Dump Rules

There are only a few, simple rules for this step. Four, to be exact.

1) Just write. The whole time allotted to this step should be spent writing. It's not time to research online, think about what order things should be in, or wonder if you should write something down or not. Just get all your thoughts on paper.

2) Don't over think. This part of creating your course is simple, so do not complicate it! Write down everything that pops in your mind about your course topic. Remember, no excessive or extraneous thinking is allowed.

3) Make sure you do it. Even if you already know what you want to include in your course, this step helps you get everything out of your head. It makes it easier for you to later organize the content. Please, do not skip this step.

Spend at least an hour jotting down everything you can think of related to the problem you're solving. No idea is too small or too big or too dumb or too farfetched.

Just get them all down on paper for now. If you like writing on paper with lines, brainstorm on lined paper. If you prefer an open space where you can let your ideas flow (maybe draw diagrams, pictures, or create a mind map), use blank paper or even a drawing pad. Feel free to print extra pages, too. The point is to get all your ideas about the topic down on paper! And with this step, I recommend not using a word processing program or any other tools available on the internet. Write until your hand hurts for best results.

Organize Your Content

In the previous step, you got all your ideas out of your head and down on paper. Now it's time to review those notes and begin to put together an outline of your course material.

You're going to get organized in a major way.

Review your brain dump notes and worksheets from the previous step and map out the lessons for your online course. Remember, index cards or sticky notes make it easy to move around your ideas, but they are not necessary.

If you do choose to use index cards, sticky notes, and/or a worksheet to organize, then line up your content in a timeline from problem to solution.

You won't be creating any additional material in this step. The objective is to simply organize your notes into a timeline and no more.

The order of the content is important. You want to make sure each step builds onto the next until your client has finished the course and achieved his or her goal.

Create a Timeline

As you think about the best order for your content, start by asking yourself what your client needs to know first? Then what comes after that? And then what's next?

Continue this process in small pieces until you've moved from the problem to the solution.

Follow these suggestions to help you complete this step:

1) Create a mental timeline from the problem you're solving to the goal your clients will achieve. Then organize your ideas along that timeline.

2) Think of each idea as a lesson. (Later on you will group the lessons into modules, but for now, focus on organizing your lessons in a linear fashion.)

3) Only write the general theme of the lesson. Don't include detailed information about each idea just yet.

4) Since you will most likely be moving lessons and ideas around, it helps to use index cards or sticky notes. Then you can easily arrange them on your desk or workspace.

5) Remove ideas that don't fit the timeline; add others as they occur. (Again, sticky notes or index cards make it easy to organize ideas in this way.)

Don't feel pressured to get the lessons in the perfect order on the first go round; there is time to do this later on as you continue with your course creation.

Outline Your Lessons

Write as many lessons as needed to take your client from where they are right now (the problem) to where they desire to be (the solution). I think of a lesson as a bite size chunk of content that stands on its own as a piece of your overall course.

To give you a general idea, your course will likely have somewhere between 12 and 30 lessons in total. If you come up with more than 30 lessons, don't worry. You can use some of your extra ideas to create bonus material.

Keep in mind that chapters don't always necessarily translate into course lessons. And sometimes the scope of the book is too large for easy-to-implement courses, if you try to teach the whole thing.

Separate Your Content into Modules

The first part of this step is to look over your lessons and make logical groupings (modules) of the lessons along your timeline.

Your aim should be to create four to six modules, each with three to five lessons.

If you used index cards or sticky notes, it is easy to physically move them around to the appropriate grouping. Indicate modules by marking lessons with different colored pens or markers.

Once you have grouped your ideas, you are ready to begin making notes about each lesson.

Now it's time to add content. If your lessons are on index cards or sticky notes, it's easy to simply add information right then and there.

The point of expanding on each idea is to prepare you for writing the actual lesson (which you'll do in the next step).

As you look over each of your lessons, write whatever pops into your mind that you don't want to forget.

Write Your Lessons

Tips for Writing Your Lessons:

1) Start with your book in hand. This is the logical place to begin repurposing your book's content into an online course.

2) Reuse and repurpose your content. You likely already have plenty of content you can repurpose, so start there. Find blog posts, eBooks, free giveaways, and other content you can use as a starting point. You may also have some PLR - private label rights - content you may use. Rewrite it about fifty percent to make it your own.

3) Schedule time. It's crucial you schedule time in your calendar to write your lessons. It is up to you whether you prefer setting aside big chunks of time (think a whole afternoon or weekend) or if you want to plan an hour every morning until it is completed. The key is to plan for your success!

4) Stay focused. When you write, stay on topic. Make sure what you are including is relevant to the lesson and module. Also, refrain from going on tangents or making a lesson longer than it needs to be. You want your lessons to be practical and easy to digest. If I digress when I am working on this step I always have to go back and redo my lessons.

5) Don't stress out about the format. This step is about creating the content; you can make it look pretty later. Focus on

getting each lesson written. You will have the opportunity to play around with style and format before you launch the course.

6) Consider including exercises and activities. Depending on the lesson you are teaching, it may help course participants to have an exercise or "homework" assignment associated with the topic. Only include one if you think it would help your clients implement the content or better understand the lesson.

Interactive courses make for more satisfied clients. Rather than just offering video or text content, consider adding fillable PDFs, quizzes, and other methods for keeping your clients interested and moving forward. Imagine their excitement as they share this experience with the people in their lives.

You don't have to include activity in every lesson or module, but what you do have to do is make sure that any interactive component you use is relevant to what was just learned. It should enhance what is being taught and help students to understand the concept or skill you are teaching more deeply. When you think back to when you were in school, it was the "hands-on" types of experience that kept you interested and continue to be the most memorable.

In the last step of this workbook you will review all your lessons.

Review What You Have Created

It is important to review the entire course content from your ideal client's point of view. You want to pretend you are her and try to solve her problem as you review the course.

Questions to Consider During Your Review:

Think about your ideal client and then ask yourself these questions as you go through the content.

1) Will she achieve her ideal goal at the end?

2) What's missing that she needs to know, do, or have in order to get there?
3) Are any of the lessons confusing, ambiguous, or unclear?
4) Does the order of lessons still make sense?
5) Are all included exercises pertinent and relevant?
6) What foundation pieces are necessary, but not included? (These will make excellent bonuses!)

Once you have gone through the course with these questions in mind, make any necessary changes. This is the time to be sure you like the order of the lessons and everything needed is provided.

Bonus Material

You can also begin thinking about what bonus material to include with the course. One great option is foundational, but not specifically relevant, material. Create a lesson about the content and offer it as a bonus.

The foundational content pieces will serve as refreshers to participants who are already familiar with the material. And if a participant has little knowledge in that area, it ensures he or she has the tools to succeed in the course.

I have also used the strategy of asking my colleagues to create or provide a relevant and related bonus to my online courses. This gives others the opportunity to be introduced to your students and enhances what you have created in a positive way.

Before launching the course, you may want to offer a beta version to a small number of clients. You can also have a team member go through the course from your client's point of view. Both options should give you helpful feedback. Then you can make further changes before your full launch.

Once you are happy with your content, you are then ready to send everything for editing and design work.

The tenth step is delivering your online course. The next chapter is devoted entirely to this part of the process of turning your book into a business.

CHAPTER 11

Deliver Your Online Course

The possibilities are nearly endless when it comes to delivering your online course, even one based on your book.

Let's break this down into five steps:

1) Which course format is right for you?
2) Creating video and/or audio courses
3) Where to host your courses
4) Workshop courses
5) Membership courses

Which Course Format?

Video, audio, interactive PDFs, live Q & A sessions, and plenty of other delivery methods and course formats are possible, so the first step is to decide what form and format you'll choose, and which software platform is the best match for your ideal participant and what you are teaching in your course.

There's a format for every learning style. First identify your ideal student's preferred learning style, as well as what type of course format you are most comfortable using. Your goal should be to put your book contents into a format that appeals to different learning styles, so that you can attract people who would love your content, but who don't like to, or have time to, read a book.

And don't assume that those who bought the book won't also want to take course. The aim is to make them want more of you and your teaching. Consider also that they may have purchased the book because at the time a course version of what they wanted to learn wasn't yet available.

The number one key for turning your book into an online course will be to assess your content and decide which format suits the material best.

If your book teaches life principles and values you may want to create an inspirational audio or video course to enhance what you taught in your book.

If your book teaches how someone may achieve a specific results or master your system, create a step-by-step course with detailed charts, diagrams, and screenshots.

If your book teaches someone how to make or create something that requires skill, create a how-to course to explain everything in great detail.

And if your book contains interviews with guest experts, create a course that contains the original audio or video interviews with your experts. You may edit these and package them as a course about your specific topic.

Creating Video or Audio Courses

Do not be intimidated by the thought of creating a course using video. I know this described my mindset when I hosted my first webinar in 2009. Once I did it a few times and asked my questions to the support team for the service I had chosen (GoTo Webinar) to get clarification, it soon became a part of how I conducted my business on the internet.

A video course is ideal for your business if both you and your target audience are visual learners. Just make sure you find out in advance whether or not video is the preferred form for your community.

If your ideal course participant is an auditory learner, or simply has a lifestyle that sees the majority of her learning done while jogging or driving, then audio courses would be a perfect accompaniment to your book.

Creating podcasts or audio book versions are both effective options. More and more authors are "teaching" their book's content through audio outlets, both paid and free.

My very first online course in 2007 consisted of three audios (I hosted this course live and then immediately put it into home study to sell more spots) and a workbook the students could download in advance. This was before I was an author and the content was not based on any book, but I wanted to share with you what is possible and how this online course format can lead to greater things for you over time. The idea is to teach what you know in a way that will benefit your audience.

Be sure to include the link to a page where the listener will be able to access the resources you provide once they are in front of a smart phone or computer. I need to emphasize the importance of making this step a simple one for those who join your course.

If you don't want to use the podcast format but instead simply present modules on a membership site or through straight digital delivery, you can also create simple audio only lesson recordings with services such as Instant Teleseminar. I know the creators of this service personally and have been a customer since they began in 2007.

Don't let all this information overwhelm you. Just be aware of the connection between your book topic and audience, and the type of course most likely to enhance the value of your book. Give yourself the time to learn and internalize what I am sharing here so that it will become second nature for you to move forward confidently.

Just as you want to keep your lessons simple, actively eliminating any non-essential material that might confuse or frustrate your student, so too do you want to make course delivery and format as simple as possible. Ultimately, that means choosing the method that resonates best with you as the author and host of your material.

Where to Host Your Audio/Video Courses

You can sell video courses directly or offer them as courses to commercial teaching platforms/marketplaces such as Udemy, Thinkific, or Teachable.

With commercial teaching marketplaces, there is often an approval process, plus limitations such as being required to sign non-disclosure agreements or restrictions on what and how you can teach.

As a positive with the larger teaching platforms, there is massive exposure and consistent marketing, plus many people looking for a course automatically search those platforms first. Fees in some form usually apply with larger platforms such as them taking a percentage of your earnings. You're compensating them for hosting your course plus having it available in their catalogue. In other words, you are paying for their popularity. If you can sell your course directly without going through a commercial course marketplace, do so. But you have to consider the pros and cons, before signing up as an instructor.

Selling Your Course Directly:

You may also sell your course directly from your website, using a payment processing method. I continue to offer my courses in this way so that I am responsible for and in control of my business.

If you are selling video course access, you will need a platform in the cloud for video storage. If you are using a webinar SaaS (Software as a Service) that includes storage, such as GoToWebinar or Zoom, your problem is already solved. You can take a live webinar, or a series of live webinars, record them and sell them as "on demand" courses.

An alternative: Creating lessons on video without the live component, recording them and using them as paid course modules.

You will need cloud storage for your online courses. If you are using a platform like Udemy, the platform usually stores your course material: Otherwise you will need a cloud storage solution such as Amazon S3. I have used Amazon S3 for a decade and find it to be a reliable and cost effective solution for my business. And even if the platform you choose will host your content as a part of your package with them, you will still want to have a backup of everything on your own cloud storage account.

Finally, there is always Facebook Live. Run (and record) livestreams as part of a paid membership group, with a closed or secret Facebook group that you can use as your platform.

Workshop Courses

Webinars make great workshop platforms. Using a webinar platform such as GoToWebinar or Zoom allows for real-time interactivity. On GoToMeeting or Zoom Meeting, the participants are able to see you and each other on screen. It has the feel of a private, intimate conference room and is the perfect delivery system for small, higher-ticket courses.

You will also be able to create one-time-only live seminars based on your books; then offer the recording on-demand.

Workshop courses are a great way to get people to put your book teachings to actual, practical use and to create a strong sense of community between you and your participants.

Membership Courses

The easiest way to host a membership-based course is to do it on your blog, using a simple WordPress plugin such as Wishlist Member or other membership solution to turn part of your site into a private platform for your courses and students.

Membership courses are great options for books that deal with an ongoing learning curve capable of carrying the reader on through several more levels of advancement. For example, books based on life skills.

Membership sites are great if you want to create and build a strong, loyal community while reaping recurring monthly income. I currently have more than fifty membership sites, with a dozen of them being based on one or more of my books.

PART IV

Using the Power of Stories in Your Book and Business

"Stories are 22 times more memorable than facts alone..."

~ Jennifer Aaker

As an author, you're probably well aware of the power of stories in books. After all, most authors are voracious readers. But you may not have thought about how useful stories are for a business. As a matter of fact, stories are crucial for creating a brand, retaining loyal customers, and inspiring new customers.

Imagine a rapt audience listening to the story of how you overcame obstacles and succeeded beyond your wildest dreams. The effect of a well-crafted, relevant story is unlike any other content you write – it has a much more emotional effect.

The chapters in this part explain how you can use stories to grow your business.

CHAPTER 12

Stories are More Memorable

"Once upon a time..."

~From most fairy tales

You can explain a principle, but if you also tell a story about it, people are more likely to remember it. We forget facts and figures, we forget principles and tenets, but we remember stories.

Jennifer Aaker, Professor of Marketing at Stanford Graduate School of Business, says "Stories are 22 times more memorable than facts alone... Studies show that we are wired to remember stories much more than data, facts, and figures. However, when data and story are used together, audiences are moved both emotionally and intellectually."

All I Remember Is Two Stories...

I majored in History in college – not for any good reason except that I liked it. I studied Russian History, the history of the American West, World War II, and much more.

That was many years ago and I recently realized how little I remembered. In fact, all I remember is two stories. One is the story of the Donner family in History of the American West. The Donner Party, or Donner–Reed Party, was a group of American pioneers that set out for California in a wagon train in May 1846. They were delayed by a series of mishaps and mistakes and spent the winter of 1846–47 snowbound in the Sierra Nevada mountains. I won't retell it here but you can look it up if you want. This story doesn't have a happy ending – it was shocking actually – as many of them didn't survive.

The other story was from my Russian History class. Tsar Peter the Great was 6 feet 8 inches tall. This was very unusual in those days. In 1697, he decided to travel "incognito" to Western Europe for 18-months with a large delegation. He used a fake name to escape social and diplomatic events, but since he was so much taller than almost anyone else, he did not fool anyone of importance. So, everyone had to pretend that they didn't know who he was!

I remember our professor painting this picture for us and thinking how funny it was. I never forgot this story. Even 40 years later, I remember the basics of these two stories.

That's the power of stories.

The Value of Attention

These days, the attention of your readers, subscribers, and website visitors is split. There are always interruptions demanding attention. Yet attention is what you need. If you can stand out from the crowd, people will remember you.

Stories help you get attention. It's our nature to pay attention to a good story. In a later chapter, we'll cover the parts of a good story.

The Importance of Emotion

You may have heard the idea that people buy on emotion and in fact, there's plenty of research showing this. Of course, people make decisions in different ways, but emotion is almost always important.

Stories are great at portraying emotion—they can be happy or sad, funny or serious, inspiring or boring. You can move people to feel the urgency and intensity of their problem more easily with a story than with facts. That doesn't mean that you shouldn't use facts, just that it's important to evoke emotion as well.

Harvard professor Gerald Zaltman wrote that 95% of purchasing decisions are unconscious and that most of the unconscious urges are related to emotion. He concludes that emotion is what really drives purchasing behaviors.

I sometimes tell the story of why my husband went out to buy two parakeets for our two sons and came back with four. They were on sale and he couldn't resist getting a good bargain. Yes, four parakeets still cost more than two and were more expensive (and time consuming) to take care of, but they were on sale!

We'll talk more about emotion in a later chapter.

CHAPTER 13

The Six Kinds of Stories You Can Tell

What types of stories can you tell for your business? Here, we're distinguishing between stories in your book and stories that you use to persuade people to subscribe or buy a product. The stories in your book will be about the content and may not be designed to be persuasive yet they'll still help your readers to remember your content better.

There are six types of stories you can tell and we explain them in the next few paragraphs.

Your Company/Brand Story

This is one of the most important stories you can tell. It's the origin story of your company or brand. Why did you start it? What problems do you solve for customers? What do you stand for? What have you accomplished? How did it happen?

This story will help you potential customers decide if they want to do business with you.

An example is the story of TOMS, which sells shoes as well as other products. While traveling in Argentina in 2006, TOMS Founder Blake Mycoskie witnessed the hardships faced by children growing up without shoes. Wanting to help, he created TOMS Shoes, a company that would match every pair of shoes purchased with a new pair of shoes for a child in need. One for One®.

The Personal Story

A personal story is a story from someone's life, usually yours. It could be how you overcame difficulties to reach the place where you are today.

Many personal stories involve overcoming difficulties. They help your potential customers feel that they can overcome their difficulties as well.

Here is one of the personal stories I tell…

Years ago, I wrote a quarterly article for the magazine Presentations – which is no longer published. In January, 2004, I wrote an article called "Presentations Without Bullets."

I created a screenshot of a slide for the article that was so ugly that a reader wrote a letter to the editor asking, "How could you publish such a bad example of a slide? It has no focus. Please, give us better examples!" And they published that letter in the magazine the following month.

As you can imagine, I was mortified, embarrassed beyond belief when I read it. So, I decided that I would learn how to design slides. I wasn't a designer, so I had to start from scratch.

I started going to a PowerPoint conference every year. I read books and I read research on what types of presentations work best. Over the years and many presentations, I figured out the techniques that I could use to help my clients succeed with their own presentations.

As a result of all my studying, in 2010, I became PowerPoint MVP. MVP is a Microsoft award, the highest award that Microsoft gives to experts in its products. MVPs have to contribute at no charge to the user community, which I do with the free content on my blog, by giving free webinars, and more. I have to reach a lot of people, which I do – my EllenFinkelstein.com website reaches about 100,000 people each month and my PowerPoint Tips newsletter goes out to about 10,000 people.

The combination of what I learned and the MVP award helped me to create a thriving business.

The value of this story is that it helps potential customers realize that if I could learn to design slides without any artistic talent, they can, too.

The Product Story

You can tell stories that relate to products. Your story could be how the product was developed, why it came into existence, a problem the product makers had to solve, or how a customer used it in a creative way. If you have one product, this might be the same as the company/brand story.

A good example of a product story is the one about the origin of the idea for the Sony Walkman. Masaru Ibuka, Sony's co-founder often travelled for business and he liked to listen to music. However, he hated dragging around a bulky cassette player. He asked his engineers to create something smaller and more portable – just for playback and for use only with headphones – and the Walkman was born. This gave us not only the Walkman, but, by extension, all of the portable music players we use today.

The Customer Story

Tell how your customers relate to your product or service. This is a great story because it emphasizes the benefits of what you offer. When people read about a customer's experience with your product or service, they put themselves in the customer's shoes and see how your products or services can benefit them.

This type of story can be similar to a case study but it's more general.

The Employee Story

Employee stories are engaging because they take your readers and viewers behind the scenes and add a human element to your company. These stories help to convey your corporate culture.

An employee story might tell how an employee improved a product or service, helped the company reach one of its goals, or bent over backwards for a customer in need.

The Case Study

A case study is a more detailed and researched story of an event in your company. The most typical one is the story of how you helped a customer improve results. For example, maybe you helped a customer increase sales by 20%.

A case study includes specific data that you can verify. A case study might be a detailed retelling of a customer or employee story.

CHAPTER 14

How to Make Stories Relevant

Stories must be relevant to your audience and readers if they are to be effective. They need to have a purpose. Another way to say this is that you need to use stories strategically, with a goal in mind.

Knowing Your Audience

The first step to making your stories relevant is knowing your audience. What do they think their problem is? What will help them solve their problem? What are their limiting beliefs that stop them from solving their problem? What objections will they come up with to stop them from buying or subscribing? What are their values and what emotions speak the most to them?

You may need to do some market research to gather your audience's demographics, such as age, economic level, location, gender and so on, as well as their psychographics. Psychographics are thoughts, feelings, opinions, values and attitudes. Some marketers pay too much attention to demographics and too little to psychographics. Attitudes and values play a very important part in storytelling. If your story is in tune with your audience, it will resonate with them.

Deciding on Your Most Effective Message

Based on your audience and your strategic goals, what is your best message? What message will draw your audience to you? What is it that you really want to say?

Your story is a way of expressing that message, a metaphor that makes your point in a more engaging and personal way.

Let's say that many of my readers want a successful online business but don't take the necessary action because of doubts or fears.

And let's say that I want my message to be that you have to learn to take decisive action if you want to succeed in your own business.

Now that I have decided on my audience and the message I want to convey, I'm ready to build my story.

CHAPTER 15

The 4 C's of Story Structure

Once you've decided on the type of story you want to tell and the message you want to give them, you are ready to write it. You can use the "4 C's" to make sure you include all the necessary elements and structure. Including the 4 C's in each story will help ensure that you have the desired effect.

Here are the 4 C's and how to use them:

1. Context

The context sets not only the location of the story but the situation the characters find themselves in. Provide some visual detail about the situation. It establishes the relevance of the story to the audience (see more about this in the next chapter).

Use the Context section to create a "hook" that captures the attention of your readers or audience. What is unusual about the situation? Think about how to create anticipation to hear the rest of the story.

2. Characters

After you set the context, you need to say something about the characters, the people in the story. They should relate to your audience in some way.

The characters have a problem or are in a situation that needs resolution. Your audience will identify with one or more of the characters in the story.

Bring your characters alive by quoting them directly or describing how they look.

3. Conflict

Focus on the conflict which is the heart of your story. The conflict or obstacle can be of ideas against ideas or people against people. Give some intensity to the conflict or obstacle that you audience can identify with.

4. Conclusion

In your conclusion, describe how the obstacle was overcome or the conflict resolved. Usually, you want your story to have a happy ending, although not always. (A story of failure can also help your audience understand what they need to do.) Remember your message? Don't assume that your audience will "get it." State the "moral" of the story clearly.

CHAPTER 16

Engaging Your Readers

We've talked about the types of stories you can tell, how to make them relevant, and how to structure them, but storytelling is an art, too. In this chapter, we'll explain some of the finer details of storytelling that will make your stories more powerful.

Create an Emotional Connection

As we've noted, a good story makes an emotional connection. Why do non-profits focus on one hungry child rather than the statistics of how many hungry children there are? Because you can't feel compassion about numbers, but you can about that one child.

Why do security companies create ads about thieves – online and in your home? That fear convinces buyers to buy security hardware and software.

Why do business coaches talk about their lifestyle? Because the desire for that lifestyle pushes people to buy their coaching.

When your story is genuine and from the heart and touches on your readers' pain, it will be persuasive. When you meet them where they are and clearly describe where they want to be, you'll get results.

When your readers can relate to the characters in your story, it keeps them riveted. They're rooting for the hero and hoping that she'll succeed. They identify with the hero, which may just be you, if you're telling your personal or company story. They want to be a hero, too.

Create Suspense and Anticipation

Suspense and anticipation are important in any story. They keep the audience glued to the story to see what will happen in the end. Although everybody knows that the children in the plastic bubble gyrosphere in Jurassic World won't get eaten by the dinosaur that's chomping on the bubble, we're glued to the screen to see what will happen.

How can you add suspense to your story? By emphasizing the risks you took or how you felt during crisis. How close to failing did you come? Although your readers know that you came out all right, they'll follow along with you if you explain the fear you felt or the doubt you experienced. They may be feeling the same fear and doubt and will be carried along with you.

Inspire People to Take Action

Stories don't have to be inspirational to be interesting – some famous stories are tragedies, after all – but for stories in a marketing context, you want to inspire your audience. Remember that hungry child? The fundraising ad isn't supposed to drive you to despair and give up hope. The conclusion is always, "You can make a difference."

Inspiration is important in marketing because it persuades people to take action. Taking action could mean buying a product, subscribing to your free offer, or sharing a blog post you wrote. Stories without hope and inspiration don't lead the audience to take action.

So after telling an inspirational story of some success you had, you can say, "If I could do this, so can you, IF you take the next step." In business, every story should have a call to action.

Let Your Personality Come Through

In whatever story you tell, your personality should play a major part. This is why marketers so often start sales webinars with some background about their personal life. Think about how your past led you to your current business and why. Then tell that story.

I told you the story of how I learned how to design slides (and teach others to design them). It started with someone complaining about how bad a slide of mine was and that spurred me to learn simple and effective methods of design. I then turned that into a method (The Tell 'n' ShowSM method) that anyone can apply.

Keep People Attentive

One effective storytelling technique is to break up the story. Instead of telling the entire story all at once, offer just the first part. This is a good way to keep your audience paying attention to hear the rest. It's like a weekly TV serial that ends on a cliffhanger. You'll come back to watch the next week to see what happens.

You might break up your story only for a few minutes in a video. On a sales page, you can start a story at the top and tell them you'll tell them more in a minute, which is really at the bottom of the page.

This technique is called creating a loop. You open the loop but don't close it right away, keeping your audience rapt because they want to hear the ending.

Create Viral Stories

Content that gets widely shared or goes viral online has one thing in common – it elicits strong emotions. These stories could be awe-inspiring, funny, moving, illuminating, inspiring, shocking, sexy, scary, infuriating or controversial. Spicing your stories up with these emotions will help your stories get liked, shared, and linked to, but make sure they're right for your brand and audience. As they say, it's always wise to avoid politics and religion!

Make Stories Visual

The more visual elements you can add into your story, the more likely it will be shared. If you're writing a book without pictures, use words to describe the scene. How did it look, smell, sound, taste, and feel?

If you can incorporate pictures and video, that's even more powerful. In fact, you can create images that tell stories without any words at all. The reason visual elements make stories more effective is that they more directly trigger emotions.

Photographs and live videos will usually do this more effectively than illustrations and cartoons because they're more realistic. A photo of a hungry child is way more touching than a drawing of one.

CHAPTER 17

Choose the Best Media for Your Story

In the last chapter, we started talking about images and video and in this chapter, we'll go a little more deeply into media because you can tell a story through any type of media, whether it's text, images, or video.

Your Story Extends Beyond Your Book

When you think about moving from a book to a thriving business, you need to understand that your story will go beyond your book. People may tell others about the stories in your book, because people love to retell stories.

You may use short versions of a story in a group coaching session, on a Facebook Live, or on a webinar. And we'll talk in a minute about using stories when speaking to a live audience – very important!

The more fundamental the lesson of your story, the more it will spread and the more places you'll be able to use it. Children's stories are good examples of this. When my children wouldn't help in the kitchen, I told them the story of The Little Red Hen. (If you don't know that story, look it up.)

Use Text to Tell a Story

Many stories are told in text. As an author, you're probably most familiar with writing a story in text. As we explained in the first part of this book, you need to plan ahead. Just as you should outline your book, you should outline your story to make sure you have included all of the components – the four "C's."

When writing your story, don't try to sound formal or overly literate. Write using an informal, personal tone that's easy for your audience to understand and relate to.

Finally, reread the story and make sure it is relevant and provides value to your readers. Will they learn something useful and they can put into action?

Use Video to Tell a Story

While text is the traditional way to tell – or write – a story, these days you have other options. One of the most powerful is video, especially if your business is mostly online and you have little access to a live audience.

Just a few years ago, creating a video was difficult and expensive. Now, it's as easy as taking out your smartphone or using your computer's webcam.

Some people are shy about using video – but you don't have to be! Here are some tips:

Make it Short and Simple

People usually watch only a few minutes. For a story, just keep it short. You can follow up with text explanation as well.

On YouTube, videos need to be especially short. Research has shown that for a video of 4-5 minutes, fewer than 60% of your viewers will still be watching compared to 75% for a 1-2 minute video. On the other hand, you can invite people to an hour-long video and if you keep it lively and relevant, most people will stay. You can sprinkle multiple stories throughout.

Use the Technology that's Most Comfortable for You

The most obvious type of video is a "talking head," in which people see you but there are other options. Examples are:

- Cartoons created with cartoon software
- PowerPoint slides (or slides created with Keynote, Google Slides, or other options)
- Screen captures, which are great for technical demos
- Later in this chapter, we'll suggest some tools you can use to create videos.

Use Images to Tell a Story

One simple image can be a powerful story. You've probably seen photojournalism that has made a lasting impression on you. Often these images are heartrending but joyful photos can also be highly impactful.

As we've mentioned, photos tend to have a more emotional effect because they're more realistic than an illustration. Nevertheless, sometimes you want to use an illustration, infographic, chart, map or diagram, especially in a more professional, business-like setting.

Tell Your Story When You Speak

Of course, we can't forget that you can TELL your story, that is, speak it out loud in front of a live audience. Use stories in your live events, such as webinars and offline events. Tell very short stories when you meet people at networking events. A short customer story can make a great elevator speech.

Find the Right Tools to Convey Your Story

These days, everything seems more highly technical than when we just spoke out stories to people in the same room as us.

Don't let a lack of resources, tools, or skills stop you from using the right medium. For example, many people think that video is hard, but as we've said, it's never been easier.

You can find tools and resources to make any kind of content creation easy, no matter what your skill level or budget.

Tools for Images

Here are some tools you can use to create and edit images and photos:

- **Fiverr:** This is a platform where you can find graphic designers (as well as editors, formatters, and more)
- **Canva:** Here you can create and edit photos and graphics
- **GIMP:** This is a free, open-source Photoshop clone.
- **Pixlr:** This is a free photo editing website
- **Snipping Tool:** This is Windows' screen capture tool. Use **Grab** if you're on a Mac
- **PowerPoint:** Many people don't realize that PowerPoint has powerful graphic editing capabilities
- **Your smartphone:** Obviously, you can take photos with your smartphone and there are many smartphone apps that let you edit them

Tools for Video

Here are some tools you can use to create and edit video:

- **iMovie (Mac) and Windows Movie Maker:** These are basic video editing tools
- **Camtasia:** This tool can do screen captures as well as powerful editing
- **PowerPoint:** You can create video in PowerPoint using its animation tools or by just creating slides and setting the timing between slides.
- **Zoom:** This is video meeting software but you can also share your screen. Just record to create a video.

- **Your webcam:** Your webcam has software that lets you create video
- **Your smartphone:** Yup, you can just use your smartphone. You might want to consider using a tripod to keep things steady. There are many smartphone apps to help you edit and format video as well.

Live Events

The tools here help you create online live events—webinars and group meetings.

- GoToMeeting and GoToWebinar
- Readytalk
- YouTube Live
- Zoom Meeting and Zoom Webinar
- Facebook Live

CHAPTER 18

Distribute Your Story

Where do you put your story? We've already referred to some of these options but it's worthwhile to delve deeper because the more places you put your story, the more people will see it.

Tell Your Story in Your Book

Obviously, you can – and should – tell your story or multiple stories in your book. You can put your origin story in your introduction or the first chapter to help people get to know you right away. You can add relevant stories throughout to keep readers interested and make your points more powerfully.

But that's not all!

Tell Your Story on Your Website and Blog

You can tell stories on your website. Besides your blog, your About page is a great page for your origin story, customer stories, and product stories.

Speaking about blog posts, think of ways to use stories often there. You'll engage people much more than with simple principles. Because blog posts are dated, you can easily use stories based on seasons, holidays, and current events.

Use Social Media to Tell Stories

Social media is a great place to tell stories. Again, seasonal material is appropriate. Tell stories about events in your life that relate to your business topic. I have a friend who is a business coach and almost every time she goes shopping, she has a lesson to tell about how the merchant did something right or wrong – and why. These personal/business stories are very effective.

Tell Stories in Emails

If you preface your emails with a very short story and relate it to what you're selling, you'll increase sales. That's because you'll draw your subscribers into the email with the story and elicit emotion from them. Think about how something you did or saw relates to the product you're selling and explicitly make the connection.

Here's an example from one of my recent emails:

"We're back in Davie, Florida and in 1-1/2 weeks, we'll be back in Iowa! I'm looking forward to seeing daffodils and tulips in my garden. Have you already seen signs of Spring?

Spring is an obvious symbol of growth and one of the best ways to grow your business is to grow your list. And one of the best ways to grow your list is to create multiple freebies to attract people to subscribe. More about that in a minute."

First, I talked about something personal and connected that to Spring. Then I connected Spring to growth. Finally, I connected plant growth to business growth.

Post on Content Sites

You need to reach beyond your subscribers, followers, website visitors and one great way to do that is to post on content sites. Two sites that often don't get enough attention from online entrepreneurs is Medium.com and Reddit.com.

- Medium is a place to publish articles. It gets millions of visitors each month and it's free to use although you can purchase an upgrade.

- Reddit is a series of topic-based groups and there's one for almost everything. Reddit can get a little raw, but in most cases, people are helpful and supportive.

There are many other possibilities, including forums for trade/industry organizations.

Everything we've said about stories applies to articles. Either start with a short story or incorporate one into the article's content.

Chapter 19

Starting Your Stories

"Successful people maintain a positive focus in life no matter what is going on around them. They stay focused on their past successes rather than their past failures, and on the next action steps they need to take to get them closer to the fulfillment of their goals rather than all the other distractions that life presents to them."

~ Jack Canfield

Now you know...
1) Why you need to use stories
2) The 6 types of stories you can tell
3) The 4 C's of story structure
4) How to know which story is most effective for your market
5) How to create a story that engages your readers
6) How to know which media to use to create your story
7) Where to distribute your story

Start with One Story and Let Them Multiply!

Now it's time to get to work on your story. Focus on just one story first. It may not be as perfect as you'd like if it's your first one, but you'll get better and better at storytelling the more you do it.

If you need help with the production side of things, you can always work with people who are experts in the skills that you lack.

Practice telling the story out loud and record yourself. Listen to the recording and you'll probably find something to tweak and improve. Then find as many places as possible to use it, in as many formats as you can.

Wishing you a happy ending!

Part V

What's Next in Your Journey

By now you can see there are many ways in which you may share your book's message with the world in general and with your target audience in specific.

We have discussed the value of building relationships with others online and offline, the importance of storytelling, the magic of teaching your information through an online course, and so much more.

In addition, we discussed the history of the book to business model, the art and science of funnels, continuing your relationships via emails, and using social media to grow your business exponentially.

We - Ellen and Connie - have created an ongoing program where you are part of a community of authors who wish to write and publish a book or a series of books on your topics and then turn this content into an income stream. We call this program the Authors! The Quick Book to Business Method™ and it could be right for you.

In the beginning of this book, in chapters one and two we introduced you to several authors who used their book to catapult them to success. These are men and women, from different walks of life and living on different continents who have achieved more than they might have ever thought possible by striving to have their message heard by those who will resonate with it best.

Decide what goal you are aiming for – wider visibility, lead generation, cementing your expert status in your book field or even simply making more money from your content. Take into account your own skills, experiences and preferences – don't decide you need to become an instructor on Lynda.com, for example, if you already have podcasting experience. Create it with equipment you already own and upload your course to iTunes (or the Apple Podcast app) instead.

Perhaps one of your end goals is to become a public speaker. I can say without hesitation you will have an advantage over other speakers once you are a published author.

As the purchaser of this book we (Connie Ragen Green and Ellen Finkelstein) wish to gift you one of the Modules from our ongoing training course. Authors! The Quick Book to Business Method™ at:
Download a full Module from our popular course at:
https://OnlineWritingProfits.com/sample
This is our Module on Creating an Online Course based on your book.

About the Authors

Ellen Finkelstein is an online entrepreneur, business coach, and presentation skills trainer. She started her career as a Teacher of the Transcendental Meditation Technique (which she still practices) and then was an Employee Benefits Manager before starting her own business.

As an author, she has written 11 published books (25 editions) for McGraw-Hill and Wiley and published 9 e-books during her 20-year career as an author. Her books have ranged from 20 pages to 1200+ pages.

Since 1999, Ellen has been helping people to present more effectively via her websites, EllenFinkelstein.com and OutstandingPresentationsWorkshop.com.

In that time, she learned a lot about Internet Marketing, which she teaches at ChangetheWorldMarketing.com. There she helps online entrepreneurs who want to make the world a better place and shows them how to reach audiences everywhere through writing and speaking—especially via webinars. She focuses on Internet marketing strategy and technology, making the complex easy, so marketers can actually take action and achieve their goals.

As an Adjunct Professor at Maharishi University of Management, Ellen has taught Web Writing, Creating a Usable Website, eBusiness, and Internet Marketing. She also provides Internet Marketing courses and coaching sessions.

You can find out more about Ellen at
ChangetheWorldMarketing.com/About

Connie Ragen Green is a bestselling author, international speaker, and online marketing strategist who is dedicating her life to serving others as they build and grow successful and lucrative online businesses. Her background includes working as a classroom teacher for twenty years, while simultaneously working in real estate. In 2006 she left it all behind to come online, and the rest is history.

She makes her home in two cities in southern California; Santa Clarita in the desert and Santa Barbara at the beach. In addition to her writing and work online, Connie consults and strategizes with several major corporations and some non-profits, as well as volunteering with groups such as the international service organization Rotary, the Boys & Girls Clubs, the Benevolent Protective Order of Elks, the women's business organization Zonta, and several other charitable groups.

As a recent recipient of the Merrill Hoffman Award, presented to Connie by the Santa Barbara Rotary Club, being honored with this award has strengthened her resolve to serve others around the world in any way she is able to by using her gifts, talents, and experiences in a positive and sincere manner.

Find out more about Connie at
ConnieRagenGreen.com

www.ingramcontent.com/pod-product-compliance
Lightning Source LLC
Chambersburg PA
CBHW060622210326
41520CB00010B/1440